Acknowledgments

From Donna

I want to take a minute and say 'Thank You' to some very important women in my life.

My mom, **Sue Wolz**: Mom, you are responsible for my lifelong love of reading. You encouraged me to read and introduced me to so many wonderful books. You always believed in me, even when I didn't deserve it. Without your love and support, I would never have attempted to co-author this book. I love you.

Katrina Chadwick Wofford: Kat, if you hadn't introduced me to the online indie book world, I would never have known it existed. I cherish our friendship and love you like a sister.

Deb: You have helped me so much these last couple of years. Your words of wisdom truly made a world of difference to me while putting this book together. Love you like a sister, Twinkie.

Allyson R Abbott: Thank you for asking me to co-author this book. It means the world to me that you had faith in my abilities. I am so glad we had a chance to meet when you were first starting your writing career. I've seen you flourish as an author and it has been a joy to be a part of your journey.

All the authors and readers I've connected with online: My life has been enriched by all the wonderful people in the online book community. I'm blessed to have you in my life.

How to Navigate the Social Media Maze

A 'Go To' Handbook

for the

Indie Author

Allyson R. Abbott
and
Donna Wolz

Copyright 2017 Allyson. R. Abbott

All rights reserved

ISBN-13: 978-1979825412
ISBN-10: 1979825416

Acknowledgments

From Allyson

A big thank you to **Donn**a for agreeing to work with me on this project and sharing her expertise. I would also like to thank my niece, **Tamara**, for helping to check the 1000s of links that are available through this book. I know it was a boring job, but you did it with a smile. Thank you.

Content

INTRODUCTION 1

    WELCOME TO HOW TO NAVIGATE THE SOCIAL MEDIA MAZE............... 1

    LIST OF ACRONYMS FOUND THROUGHOUT THIS BOOK. 9

    THE BOOK ITSELF. 11

SECTION 1: GENERAL INFORMATION 15

    SO, HOW CAN YOU PROMOTE YOUR BOOK?...................................... 30

    WEBSITE AND BLOG TIPS 33

    USEFUL INFORMATION AND TIPS FOR ALL SOCIAL MEDIA SITES 35

    IN PERSON (INCLUDING PAPERBACKS).. 39

SECTION 2: MAKING A PLAN 43

    MAKE A PLAN:.. 44

    SET GOALS... 45

    SO, LET'S START WITH BUILDING A BRAND....................................... 48

    CATEGORIES AND KEYWORDS 56

SECTION 3: TOOLS AND TECHNIQUES 61

    FINDING THE RIGHT TOOL FOR THE JOB 61

    DOCUMENT MANAGEMENT IN THE 'CLOUD' 61

SECTION 4: SOCIAL MEDIA 81

    FACEBOOK... 84

    HOW TO GET THE MOST OUT OF USING FACEBOOK........................ 89

FACEBOOK PROMOTIONAL ACTIVITIES 106

BOOKBOTS BOB AND BILL 107

TWITTER 110

GOOGLE PLUS (G+) 132

PINTEREST..140

LINKEDIN 146

SECTION 5: CATALOGING & SOCIAL NETWORKING SITES 151

WATTPAD...155

GOODREADS AND LIBRARYTHING..159

OTHER AUTHOR AND BOOK LISTING PLATFORMS TO CONSIDER 176

SECTION 6: S M MANAGEMENT SYSTEMS & OTHER TOOLS. 179

TOOLS FOR MANAGING SPECIFIC SOCIAL MEDIA PLATFORMS 194

CROWD SPEAKING PLATFORMS ON SOCIAL MEDIA 199

SECTION 7: PROMOTIONAL ACTIVITIES............................... 205

FACEBOOK PROMOTIONS 206

OKAY, LET'S LOOK AT PROMOTIONAL ACTIVITIES ON FB. 210

HOW TO PLAN A FACEBOOK EVENT, PARTY OR TAKEOVER 214

EVENTS ORGANIZED AND HOSTED BY YOU......................................218

NEGATIVES OF HOSTING AN EVENT YOURSELF 218

EVENTS THAT OCCUR ON FB, BLOGS AND TWITTER 231

OTHER PAID PROMOTION OPPORTUNITIES......................................243

A WRAP-UP OF PROMOTIONAL ACTIVITIES 251

HOW ELSE CAN I PROMOTE MY BOOKS OR GAIN FOLLOWERS? 252

SOME FINAL WORDS OF WISDOM	284

GLOSSARY OF TERMS 293

ABOUT ALLYSON 311

ABOUT DONNA 315

Introduction

Welcome to How to Navigate the Social Media Maze.

Are you a published author or an aspiring author? Are you trying to find the best ways to utilize Social Media and other available sources? Maybe you need to learn more about promoting and building confidence to help within the social media realm before you dive in. It can be time-consuming and extremely frustrating on your own when trying to publicize your books and get your name noticed. Well, we are here to help you.

It may be that you have read *'How to Navigate The Path from Writing to Publishing'* and are keen to understand the next part of the journey, or this book caught your attention when it was promoted on Social Media (SM), or it was recommended by a friend. However you discovered this book, you will be glad you did.

We want to be perfectly clear: We are not making any outrageous promises that you will become fabulously rich and famous in a few months by following our advice. We certainly aren't offering a magic formula. We wrote this book to:

- Make it easier for you to promote your books by offering sound advice
- Provide thousands of links to resources so you won't have to spend valuable time searching for them
- Explain the pros and cons of different SM sites
- Clarify the different types of Promotional Activities
- Offer help if you need it
- Give you enough information to set you on the right path to Navigate the Social Media Maze

We believe that by using the information in this book, and with a lot of hard work, you *can* become a successful indie author.

First, we will briefly introduce ourselves and explain why we are confident we can help you. I (Allyson) am an Independent Author (indie author) from the UK, although I travel a lot. I am now living in Spain, with my husband, for the sun and enjoyment of their culture. I wrote my first short story, a fiction book, in 2014 while traveling around the USA in a motorhome. My husband and I came up with the crazy idea that writing and publishing books would top up our income to support our nomadic way of life. It seemed a simple and straightforward plan. With the writing complete, the book formatted and then published by my husband, it occurred to us that if we did not promote the book, nobody would know it was available to buy. So started my journey through the confusing maze. Not only was it a maze of the unknown, it was also an extremely intimidating maze, full of authors and readers expressing their worldly knowledge, groups of people who all seemed to know each other, bestselling and award-winning authors with thousands of followers.

I had no idea where to start, or what some of the conversations were even talking about. What was a takeover? A virtual blog tour? A hashtag or circle? The only social media platform I was aware of, and participated in, was Facebook. And that was to allow my family and friends to follow us on our travels.

This new virtual journey has turned out to be just as wondrous and amazing as our road trips. I have learned so much, made so many good friends online across the globe and built a new confidence about my abilities. This new network of friends is the most supportive group of people you will ever find. Authors, and especially indie authors, share ideas and give up their precious time to help each other, all while encouraging new authors to not give up, to believe in their own abilities.

For my part in this book, I will be sharing my valuable, time-saving information with those of you who may be published but haven't found your own footing yet in the promotion pit, or who are a little hesitant to try different platforms because you don't fully understand the rules or terminology. Also, if you don't know where to go to find available help and support, then you have wisely chosen our book.

My aim is to answer the questions you didn't know you had. To preempt that 'I am lost' feeling, and to help you see all authors are human. They are not gods or goddesses because they are 'bestselling' or 'award-winning'. I am lucky to be able to claim both of these titles. Proclaiming our awards is not used for showing off but as a marketing tool. Believe me when I say, we all need and use as many tools as we can get our hands on.

Now over to Donna Wolz, who has helped and supported indie authors to promote their books through Wise Owls PR for a good few years.

Welcome! I'm so glad you've decided to read our book. I'm Donna and I own Wise Owls PR. I've been an avid reader since I was a little bitty kid. Life is so much more fulfilling when we allow books to take us away on so many adventures, wouldn't you agree?

I love helping and promoting authors. I know indie authors don't make a ton of money and need help promoting their books, and realize it can take years for them to see the fruits of their labor bloom. Since I have had success and truly enjoy helping others to promote, I want to help you, too. If you are new to the indie book community on Social Media, you will be amazed by how many good people are willing to help you promote your books.

Social Media can be tricky to navigate and there are so many things to be aware of as you start using Social Media to let the world know about you and your book(s). I had no idea what I was doing when I first became part of the online indie book world. I asked so many questions (some of which I was sure others considered ridiculous.) I paid close attention to what everyone said and then implemented the information that worked for me. I also made numerous mistakes. In this book, I am going to share some of the things I've learned and how to avoid some of the mistakes I made. My information is not the only way to do things. It is simply what I have learned through trial and error works best for me. It is also what I have been told works for others as well.

I became involved in the indie book world several years ago when a long-time friend encouraged me to check it out. I was immediately hooked. I started to review and promote for an established blog where I learned so much. Then that same dear friend and I started our own blog. That was when I realized there was so much more I needed to learn. It was fast paced and sometimes stressful, but a fun and rewarding experience. I met so many amazing people. Sadly, due to health reasons, we had to close the blog after a year.

Shortly after our blog was up and running, I started my own business, Wise Owls PR. I had already been proofreading for a few authors and decided I wanted to get more involved in that aspect of the book world. Later, I expanded to include more options. Through Wise Owls PR, I offer various services including, but not limited to:

- Proofreading and minor editing
- I design images: banners, teasers, etc.
- I host online events
- I help promote authors
- I am also a PA/VA

I've found indie authors, and the readers who follow them, are some of the nicest, friendliest, most helpful people you will ever meet. I have made so many wonderful friends since I joined the book-related SM world-- both authors and fellow readers-- and I cherish these friendships.

I want to say Thank You for giving me the opportunity to share my experience and to offer some insight into building a following and promoting your book(s) and you on SM. I am confident that together, with this book and your dedication, you will learn how to navigate the self-publishing maze to achieve your success.

My wish for you is that you will make your dream a reality and become a successful author

List of acronyms found in this book.

ARC: Advanced Reader Copy

AZ: Amazon

B&N: Barnes & Noble

FB: Facebook

GR: Goodreads

HTML: Hyper Text Markup Language

KU: Kindle Unlimited

LT: LibraryThing

MS: Manuscript

NYT: New York Times

PA/VA: Personal Assistant/Virtual Assistant

PB: Paperback

PR: Public Relations (Promotional Resources)

SM: Social Media

ST: Street Team

TBR: To Be Read

WIP: Work in Progress

Allyson R. Abbott & Donna Wolz

The Book Itself.

It was difficult to know how to organize this book.

Although social media is the main thrust, authors also need to understand everything available to them and how to use it, the jargon used, and other aspects of the industry. With that knowledge, they can then decide which is the best route and method for them. It will all depend on budget, time, focus and goals.

Some authors bypass all the social media interactions and use paid promotions, algorithms, keywords, link placement, etc., to gain notice and sales. There is nothing wrong with that, it is just a different method. However, the majority of authors don't have the money to rely solely on paid promotions. Plus, most authors enjoy the interaction and support of the wider community and their readers, and to do this in a virtual world, you need social media. Years ago it would have meant physically going from town to town and doing signings at book shops. So, if you are heading into the social maze, the first thing you need to do is look at SM as your friend, not to be feared, but to be embraced.

We have decided that FB takes the main stage since this is where most indie authors interact with readers and other authors. Some **social media platforms** are more one-way communication, or perhaps not as well known. However, having a presence on a few platforms can be important. It is good to find out what each platform can do for you and how you can get the best out of it, as well as what the different terminology means and how to get started.

We will be:

- Discussing different promotion methods in general
- Techniques and strategies for different approaches
- Delving into the workings of various social media platforms and readers platforms
- Providing ideas on how to cope with all this extra work
- Supplying a glossary of terms

Along with all this help and information, we also have our page on FB, Author Promotion & Support with Paragon and Wise Owls PR, where you can go and ask for help, have some fun, join in an event, etc. Our FB page is specifically organized to help authors network and gain new readers or to sign up for one of the author services offered by Wise Owls PR.

The Facebook page can be found HERE

Wise Owls PR can be found HERE

My (Allyson's) husband and I also support authors through an easy and great value book award competition Paragon Book Awards (and Flash Fiction Competition) see HERE. We are always looking for great ways to support the winners, and this FB page came about when we decided that new authors needed help with social media platforms to learn the ropes and gain confidence. Therefore, the FB page is sponsored by Paragon Book Awards and Wise Owls PR. We are both there to help support the promotion of your books, and your efforts to network. We are also available to answer any questions you may have.

We do hope you enjoy this book and find value in the help we offer to guide you through the maze with a lot less difficulty than we both experienced when we started out.

Allyson R. Abbott & Donna Wolz

Please Note:

Throughout the book you will see **bold-print words.** They will be briefly explained in the glossary at the back of this book and in full on the website HERE

A complete list of all the hyperlinks used in this book can be found on our website, along with literally thousands of Facebook group links for book promotion or blogging.

Section 1:
General Information

The Ins and Outs of Book Promotion

Publishing a book, especially your first book, has an air of finality about it. At last, I've finished, the end, the book is published, hooray! You pop the cork on the bottle of bubbly feeling smug, take a deep breath, sit down and put your feet up. Job done!

Unfortunately, unless you have a big fat advance check from a publisher, or you are publishing for accomplishment and not money, this is only the start of your journey. You will now need to promote your book to get it noticed by readers. There are thousands of books published every week and yours is just one of them. You need to have a plan. No, you need to have already made a plan and been promoting your book all along.

For those who have read the first book in the *How To* series (*How to Navigate the Path from Writing to Publishing*--which from now on will simply be called The Path), you will know the importance of building a **social network**. I believe I ranted on about it quite a bit. It really is imperative to build a strong social network to promote your books.

Building a **social media network** is one of the most important things you will need to do as an author, apart from writing the book. Although I am harping on about social media, just to be clear, a social media or author platform can include newspaper articles, speaking events, radio, podcasts, television appearances, and more. It is any means you can use--whether it's a one-off or on a regular basis--to be seen or heard to promote you and your books. The more you are seen or heard, the more interest you will get. Think 'squeaky wheel!'

You should start the process of building such a platform as soon as you pick up the pen to write. There is so much information out there, and so many lovely people willing to help, offer advice, and share tips. Plus, there are thousands of eager readers, all looking for new and exciting authors. Through social media, these readers enjoy finding new books to love and sharing their finds with friends. There are hundreds of **groups**, **circles**, **followers,** and friends you didn't know you had, waiting to support your work.

If you think about it, when you are listening to a local radio show and hear about a local author, wouldn't it spike your interest? Would you also tell a friend or family member about a 'local celebrity'? Everything you do as an author will attract some attention.

Even if you don't like **Facebook**, or distrust those 140 characters on **Twitter** (which I believe are being increased to 280), you do need them. You need to embrace them, along with other communication methods. You need a platform, be it a website, a blog or a **newsletter**. You need to become visible from the very beginning. Just using the places mentioned keeps your audience limited. You need to be spreading your wings while you spread the word about your great books.

If you are thinking of starting a blog or website then check out these links to help you decide.

Helpful links

Blogspot v Wordpress 2017

Wordpress or Blogspot

Differences between wordpress.com and wordpress.org

WordPress.com vs WordPress.org

WordPress.com and WordPress.org

Cost vs Limitations vs Copyright vs Features

WordPress.com vs WordPress.org

You could of course even try selling and promoting from your own website, without uploading your books to major retail stores, but that would be a huge gamble.

Helpful link

Send Owl

How to Navigate the Social Media Maze

When promoting your book, it is also important to know where your target audience spends their spare time. You need to work out who you are writing for; women 30-50 years? Teenagers 15-18 years? Men 25-60 years?

You need to do some research to discover the main reader demographics of your genre, so you can then focus your marketing and promotional strategies toward the social media platform they are most likely to use-- even if it's not one you normally use yourself. Spend some time finding out where your target audience buys their books, in what format, and what device they read on. Do they use a tablet, computer, or smartphone? This will not only help you to target your promotions, but will show you the best format for your books so the reader has the best reading experience possible.

Check out these links to get better insight into some very useful statistics about the USA reading public.

Helpful Links

[Social Media Marketing statistics 2017](#)

[USA Book and Readers statistics](#)
has various charts to study

[USA genre popularity](#)

[Social media demographics 2017](#)

[USA Reading statistics 2016](#)

[YA and NA Information](#)

[Romance fact and figures](#)

I was a little slow on the uptake for marketing and wish I knew then what I know now!

I was that person sitting there sipping the bubbly wondering why my book was not selling. I couldn't understand it. I had written a good book, published it with a (maybe not so good) cover and the blurb said it all. So where were the sales and readers? I even chose great timing, a short love story about Valentine's Day, published at the end of January. Perfect!

Just out of curiosity, I have taken a look at the sales for that book (on AZ) in January and February of the year it was published. Wait for it…a grand total of five ebooks were sold. The irony is, this short story was written and published as a sampler for my style of writing and was supposed to be gaining me visibility for the publication of my much longer book due out in late February. What a laugh. That was my idea of a springboard, my launching pad.

This grand entrance masterpiece, that was going to make me rich, went on sale as planned in February. A total of six ebooks sold through February and March. I was already working on my next book. However, I now realized my marketing plan was not working and needed a lot tweaking!

It was at that point I started to do some research to find ways to promote books and, lo and behold, I discovered this whole new world out there on social media.

Getting sales and good reviews made me realize that my books are readable and enjoyable. I now actually have a fan base. This was all due to me climbing out of my comfort zone and sticking my neck into the promotion pot; forcing myself to mix with other authors and to chat with readers.

I was also forced to do the most un-British thing ever, and that was to blow my own trumpet, to shout about what a great book it was, to persuade others to look at me and read my work. I was so nervous and intimidated, being among bestselling authors, authors of note and so many other great books. But I did it, and so can you.

One of the best things that happened to me, and I am not sure how it came about, was I noticed a '**shout out**' for a possible **anthology.** The organizer was looking for romance books. I submitted my book and it was accepted. All of a sudden, I was working with NYT bestselling, and other award-winning, authors on the same project. We all had the same goal and we all needed to pull together to make it work. I was scared to write any posts in our secret group, in case I made myself look foolish. I watched and learned for the first week or so, only asking questions when needed. It was through observing that I noticed other authors were also feeling vulnerable and wondered if they were up to the standard required for the boxed set. I realized that most of us had reservations about our work and were insecure.

I also noted that I knew answers to some of the questions, whereas some of the others in the group didn't understand certain elements of social media or publishing, or couldn't help out with the tasks required. I have always been a 'have a go' person, so I stepped up to the mark and took the bull by the horns. I became an active member and took on a lot of the promoting responsibilities and helped other authors when possible. Suddenly, I was being looked to for answers and suggestions. We all have different strengths and weaknesses, and I used mine to help as much as possible. It built up my confidence so much that a few months later, I organized an anthology, and had the courage to invite other authors whom I had never met before.

The moral of this tale is: you may think everyone knows a lot more than you, but they may just know different things. Pooling knowledge makes a stronger group, and that is the basis of the indie author movement. Everyone shares, everyone learns and everyone wins.

So let's move on to promotion.

Although this book is mostly about the use of SM platforms, it would be very remiss of us not to look at other methods of promoting you as an author, as well as getting more sales for your books and communicating with readers.

A lot of promoting you can do yourself, for free, on **Facebook, Twitter, Pinterest, Google+,** etc. We will expand on these later. The problem is you need to reach even further and capture people outside your circles as well. This is particularly true when you are new or at the bottom of the ladder and your circle of followers or your network is fairly small and probably full of family and friends. You need to get your book in front of thousands of people who have never heard of you, and the only way to do that is to sit hour after hour posting on social media, or pay someone to do it for you..

Promoting is going to cost you money. There is no getting away from that. In fact, in the beginning, you may even spend more money on promoting than you get back in **royalties**. For example, you have a great book and have decided to price this book at 99c, which is very cheap. You need people to read your work and enjoy it so much they are willing to pay more for your next book. On AZ, if you sell your book at 99c you get 35% royalty. That's right. So for every book you sell you get 35c.

Let's break that down: If you spend $10 on a promotion, you will need to sell 29 books to break even.

The problem is, there are no $10 promotional offers that can guarantee you will get that many sales. In fact, there are no promotional packages that can guarantee you any sales.

Therefore, when you spend money promoting your masterpiece, think of it as an investment. An investment in your next book or books; an investment into your future as an author. Do your research and find the best places to invest your money. We have provided a very long list of promotion websites to get you started (link in section 7).

Of course, you might not think that 99c is a fair price for all those hours of writing, editing, formatting, creating a cover and publishing. You would be right--- it is not a fair price.

You can price your book at whatever you like, if it's a good book and it has good publicity, it will sell. I sell most of my fiction books at 99c, mainly because they are not full length. Also because I write romance and there is a lot of competition out there. I know of authors who sell their books for much more and have fewer pages, so each to their own. That is one of the joys of being an independent publisher. With that being said, most readers are unwilling to pay very much for an author's debut book.

Helpful link

How much do you charge for your ebook?

How to Navigate the Social Media Maze

No matter what you charge for your book, or where you promote, hopefully, you will find readers who not only buy your first book, but also your next book as soon as it is released. And, fingers crossed, they will also leave you a nugget of gold--- 'a book review'--- the Holy Grail for all authors.

Book reviews are as important as sales. They are social acceptance of your book. Readers share their thoughts which helps other readers choose whether to read it or not. Think about your own buying experience. Do you prefer to buy books that other readers have recommended? Or do you buy books based solely on the blurb or the author?

Our next book in this 'Calling all Authors' series is 'The Road to Building Reviews', so keep your eye out for that coming soon, or sign up for my newsletter HERE and I will let you know when it's available.

So there you have it, the five most important things an author needs to do:

- Get book sales
- Get book reviews
- Gain visibility
- Gain friends and followers
- Expand your network and social media platform

You can throw money at the issue to try and speed up the process, but if you are budget conscious and in no hurry, there are ways you can do it for free. However, the time/money balance, as well as patience, tends to run a bit thin. Do you spend your time promoting or writing your next book, which is already clogging up your brain cells and clamoring for release?

My advice, decide on a budget and try to stick with it. It is very easy to get sucked into the promotional hoopla and expect huge sales from each email sent or **blog tour** completed. But you need to be realistic and keep your expectations limited. If you succeed, then brilliant, great, well done and whatever you were doing, do it again on a bigger platform and build your following. You will spend more time promoting your books than you do writing them because there is no end in sight. The more books, the more promoting you will need to do. So, as previously mentioned, embrace it, don't fight it, because you will waste too much energy doing so

Some authors have a **PA** to help and others have managed to form a **'street team'** (more on this later) and some even have their family members helping them out. The majority of authors are left to battle the minefield on their own. If anyone offers you help, take it.

So, how can you promote your book?

There are a lot of websites and FB groups where promotional aspects of being an author are discussed, analyzed or services offered. On these, you can usually get help and advice, although some are free other you may need to subscribe and pay an annual fee.

I have included a few links. There are so many I can't include them all in this book but I have listed a few here as examples and more are available on the website HERE.

Helpful links

Writers Boon

Indie Writes

Indie Writers Support

Indie Author News, Tips and Resources

Writers Helping Writers

I visited lots of websites to try and gain insight, I bought books to learn the secrets, watched videos and podcasts. However, after all my time researching, I decided that we all have different ideas, ethics, and approaches. We all need to do what we are most comfortable with.

Most of the authors or help I read about, were either non-fiction authors (who have a slightly different approach) or their books served a purpose (mostly aimed at authors) and were published during the new exciting period of indie authors, so their words were followed by amazement by indie author wannabies (like myself).

The other type of information came from bestselling fiction writers, who used new technology like **Skype**, **blogs**, **video** and now **podcasts** to interact with their readers and then used their knowledge of these techniques and trained other authors to do the same. Consequently, they became even more popular through their training schemes than their fiction books.

If you want to investigate the Podcast route, take a look at these to get you started.

Helpful links

Authors: 4 tips for podcasts
Podcasts: Discovering a new audience
Podcasting to sell books

Most authors will create either a website, or blog, or simply use Facebook as their main way to interact with readers. Creating a website or a blog is a long way from actually getting lots of followers or readers to interact with these pages. You will end up needing to promote your page and find ways of gaining followers. It is a vicious cycle, but it's all worth it in the end.

Website and Blog tips

If you create a website, then here are some tips to make sure it is user-friendly and attracts readers:

Websites

- Create a unique design and logo---incorporate your brand
- Make it attractive
- Keep it neat and organized
- Easy to navigate
- Author bio with links to SM sites
- Obvious links to contact you
- Post your book covers and buy links
- Easy to find link to subscribe to your newsletter and, or blog. It is a good idea to have this on each page.
- Spotlight your new books and your WIP
- Spotlight Giveaways, upcoming SM events, Book signings, etc.
- Include a blog as this allows you to talk about your books, writing process, life, etc.

- (Optional) Section highlighting other authors in your genre. This gives you an opportunity to help other authors.

If you have a blog and not a website, then the same rules apply. Keep it clean and simple but appealing.

You need to build a following on your website or blog. You can do this with regular, interesting features, giveaways and promotion of your books. Interact as much as possible and always reply to any posts that your readers make.

Apart from websites and blogs, social media platforms will be the main thrust of your promotion aims. We will be going into more detail in later sections explaining how these different platforms can be used in different ways. We will also try to demystify some of the terminology.

Here are some general rules and tips from Donna, to take into consideration when you start to build your platform.

Useful Information and Tips for All Social Media Sites

- SM is the easiest, fastest, and cheapest way to promote your books, giveaways, events, and contests to an international audience.

- On all SM sites, only spend about 15% of your time promoting your books. Follow authors you like and promote their books. Engage in conversations that are non-book related with a variety of people. Like and share interesting articles, images, videos, advice, etc., that you feel your followers will enjoy. If they relate to the theme of your book, that is even better.

- Keep your posts fresh and timely.

- Be as upbeat as possible. This makes you more approachable. This doesn't mean you can't mention a problem or illness or talk about a loss, etc. Reader's want to know what is happening in your life.

- Concentrate on SM sites you are most comfortable with and really like. You are more apt to use a site if you enjoy using it.

- Make sure your bio is on each site you use. It should tell a little about you and a little about the books you write. It should also clearly state in the beginning that you are an author.

- For a username, use your name or something that followers will identify as you.

- Sometimes, there is an 'About' section in addition to your 'Bio'. Typically, you can only write a few words. Be sure you mention you are an author.

- Always add a profile picture and banner image on all SM sites that allow you to post these images. Leaving them blank looks unprofessional.

- Make sure your profile photo depicts you in a good way. If the picture is poor quality, people are more apt to ignore your profile.

- Be creative. Unique ideas are more likely to be noticed and remembered.

- Don't overuse **hashtags**. Use only relevant ones.

- Your message should always be aimed at your target audience.

- Engage your followers by asking their opinions concerning different aspects of your work. They can help you choose a name for a character, or decide where the story takes place, choose which book cover is more appealing, and the list goes on and on.

- When you post, ask a question. People are more apt to comment instead of simply *'liking'* the post. This gives you the opportunity to learn about your followers.

- Always respond to comments on your posts and any posts in which you are *'tagged'*. By acknowledging the comment, you are engaging with the person and creating a relationship.

- Find authors who write books similar to yours. Get to know them. Most indie authors are very friendly and will answer questions for you. If you join a group of like-minded authors, you can share support, encouragement, and helpful advice.

- Be on the lookout for bloggers, reviewers, cover designers, tour hosts, anyone who can help you as you navigate the world of indie authors.

- On all SM sites, be sure to spread your posts over a period of time instead of all at once. Too much at once is overload and fills up your 'followers' notifications list.

- Paying for SM advertising isn't going to be very effective if you aren't engaging with your readers. If people don't know who you are, they aren't as likely to pay attention to an advertisement.

- Publishers are more apt to take you seriously if you have been successful in building a following on SM. Don't be afraid to share that information.

- Be real. No one can keep up a facade for long before people start seeing that you are fake. If people think you are phony, they won't continue to interact with you or buy your books.

- NEVER BE RUDE! It will spread like wildfire across SM.

- Avoid drama of any kind. Getting involved in SM drama can hurt your reputation, cause you to lose followers, and lead to trolls creating havoc on all your SM sites. **Trolls** will likely trash your books and post one-star reviews.

In Person (including paperbacks)

Since most of the above has been about the internet and the best way to take advantage of it, I thought I would just mention that if you do have some paperback copies, you can actually venture outdoors and try a little footwork. I have never actually done this because I am never in the same place for long, but if I move back to the UK, it will be on my to-do list.

You can try the local hands-on approach. Local newspapers and radio shows love to chat with local celebrities. Even if you don't see yourself as a celebrity, people from your town or village will enjoy hearing about you. You could visit a few local libraries, book shops, or maybe a market stall and ask about readings, signings or question times. Have a few paperback copies printed through a print-on-demand publisher ready to give out; signed of course!

Get the local radio stations involved and plan a week or two publicity drive. If your book has a particular theme you could even try a publicity stunt, a costume, a sandwich board, a sponsored book read; anything to gain publicity.

Write an article and send it to the local paper or contact the paper to see if they would like to do an interview. If they have a section devoted to human interest/local events they should be open to talking with you.

While on the subject of the media, it is also a good idea to have a media kit handy.

What is a media kit?

It is a promotional tool to showcase you and your books. It is not the same thing as a media kit for a company. For a company, you need to include information like sale statistics, which aren't needed for authors.

An author media kit should include, at a minimum:

- Your book cover
- Synopsis
- Buy links
- Teasers/ or promotional banner
- Author bio with profile picture

- Links to your SM sites
- Tag-line, or snippets of reviews

Include anything you feel will grab the attention of readers to convince them to buy your books. They are handy to have because you will need to send them to any **PR group**/FB group promoting your book. If you contact a newspaper, radio station, library, etc., a media kit can be included.

If a blogger or book reviewer with their own website has accepted an **ARC** to review, then sending a media kit along with the ARC will allow them to use the information when they post their review on their site. Giving them access to a media kit is always a good idea, even if it is just a link to your website where they can access more promotional material.

You can send ebooks or PB books for review purposes, but make sure you know which the receiver prefers. Very few authors send paperbacks due to the cost involved.

It is a promotional tactic to publish your PB version first. Reviews can then be posted for the paperback, so place the ebook on pre-order. Buyers will see the book has reviews and hopefully purchase the ebook. When the ebook is finally published and has lots of pre-orders and reviews in place, it should hit the top ranks within days, if not hours.

You can put a book on pre-order at AZ up to ninety days before it is published. B&N allows you to place a book on pre-order for an unlimited number of days. Kobo and iBooks don't appear to have any guidelines for pre-orders. Take advantage of pre-orders so you will have sales on release day.

Now that you have all this basic information, it's time to figure out how to make it work for you. Next up is Making a Plan and Setting Goals.

Section 2:
Making a plan

Working out how to promote your books will take time. You need to make a plan. Using SM can suck hours out of a day before you realize it. As an author, I very often ignore the internet for hours, just so I can write. Replying to an email or a message on FB is never a minute or two, it always leads to something else.

Donna has some words of wisdom to share with you before you begin to get too far into this book:

This is not a step-by-step plan filled with details. It's a generalized plan to get you moving in the right direction. It's one-size-fits-all because it allows you to plug in your own details to make a plan that works for you and your circumstances. Every author has different responsibilities, strengths and weaknesses, time constraints, budget, and goals, so your plan should reflect those things.

Make a plan:

- Determine how much time you can spend dealing with SM. This includes the time it takes to set up accounts on multiple SM sites, as well as the time you will spend once the site is set up and active. Figuring out how much time you have is trickier than it seems because SM has a way of drawing us in, and before we know it, several hours have passed. Think about this carefully. I know I spend too much time on SM if I'm not careful. When I do, I don't get much accomplished.

- Which SM sites do you currently use? Are they enough or do you need to add others?

- How knowledgeable are you with using SM? Do you know how to effectively use SM or do you need time to learn how to use it? Can you figure it out on your own or do you need to find/pay someone to help you?

- Do you have the ability to make images, videos, etc.? How much time will it take you to create these things? Or do you need to pay someone to make them for you?

- Most importantly, how much money can you spend? You need to set a budget and stick to it as much as possible. You don't want to struggle financially because you didn't stick to your budget.

Set Goals

- What do you want to accomplish from using SM? You need to set goals in order to see if your plan is a success. If you set a goal of making $50/month from book sales, you have an identifiable result you can use to measure success.

- Keep your goals simple. If they are complex, it will be harder to determine how you achieved success.

- Set only one or two goals. If you set too many, you are setting yourself up for failure. Start slow and build from there.

- If you achieve your goal, how do you know it was because of your plan? Ask your followers where they first heard about your books and whether or not it caused them to buy your book. Examine the number of followers you gained and comments you have received. How often did your readers share your posts? Look at all aspects of your SM to determine how/if they helped you achieve your goal.

- If you didn't achieve your goal, follow the same steps as outlined above. Rethink your plan and make changes based on what you discovered.

- Once you achieve a goal, set a new one. Always keep reaching for the stars.

- Keep your goals realistic. They should require you to work to attain them, but not be so hard that you become frustrated and give up.

Essentials of SM success:

- Make your posts unique and different;
- Relate to your audience;
- Keep your posts short and to the point.

The better you are at these three things, the better your chances of achieving your SM goals.

Okay, now you have a plan and goals, let's see where you can spend your time and/or money.

There are basically three approaches to promotion and marketing:

- Short and sharp- lots of promotions and publicity around the publication or promotion dates
- Long and consistent promotion: regular use of SM sites, newsletters, branding, and publicity events over weeks/months/years
- A mixture of both: short bursts around new releases and price drops and then daily/weekly

> or regular promoting of books to keep them in the spotlight as much as you can.

All of these methods can be done for free, or you can pay someone to do them for you. You are more likely to see better results faster if you pay for the services of experienced people who have ways and means of contacting thousands of readers quickly. You can then do the long-term plugging yourself, once the book has had a good launching pad.

Remember, nothing is guaranteed. You can pay for a four-week tour and get zero sales, you could do a one day boost and get twenty or hundreds of downloads. You never know who will see the book and when. It all comes down to being in the right place at the right time, although some promotion platforms have better reach and results than others, so invest wisely.

The reader needs to be attracted to your book in the first place, before they will even consider checking it out further. Your cover is the most important feature of the book. The cover is more than a title and a name; it is going to be your brand.

So, Let's Start with Building a Brand

Branding

It is important to develop a brand for you and your books. A brand covers several different areas. Your name, a logo you use consistently, the font used on book covers, the style and color of book covers, and a tag-line. I did not do this when I first published my books and have regretted it ever since. Last year I got new covers for all my books and started to build a new 'look'. Now I even include a logo on my fiction book covers and Donna uses her hand-drawn owl.

How to Navigate the Social Media Maze

Components of Branding:

Your name: Use the same font for your name everywhere you can, especially on your book covers. Use the same color if possible. People may not even realize it, but they begin to recognize it as your signature style.

Logo: Create a logo to use on your SM sites. It can be anything: stylized initials, stylized name, an object, a phrase, or any combination of these. It can be related to the types of books you write, the type of characters you write about, or just something you like. Just be sure you like it enough to use it everywhere. Here are a couple of examples:

Your cover: In a series, your covers should be similar. This ensures when anyone sees a cover, they connect it to the series. Each series can have a different look but if you can continue with a theme, it will make your brand even stronger. They can be similar in myriad ways. Keep the same font, font size, font color, and/or word location the same. If you use a cute couple, a sexy man, an outdoor scene, or whatever, use a similar picture for the rest of the covers. If you use a border, they should all have borders. Is there a tag-line on one cover? Put a tag-line on all of them. Keep them as similar as possible. This shouldn't be too difficult since books in a series all have something in common.

If at all possible, keep ALL of your covers as similar as possible. This can be tricky if you write in different genres. At least keep each book cover within a genre as similar as possible.

Here are some examples:

 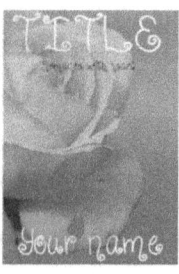 

The first 2 covers have a similar image. The font and color are the same, as well as placement of the title and your name. There is also a tag-line beneath the title on both book covers. These are all design elements that would cause readers to recognize a book as yours before they even see your name. The third cover has nothing in common with the others. While there is nothing wrong with it, there are no design elements to cause a reader to recognize it as yours.

The next four books are from two different series, but it would be hard to tell at a glance. The author, Eleanor Meyers, has branded her books through images, fonts, and bright colors. Even if your ereader does not have color, you can see the similarities.

A D Ellis, on the other hand, shows a great example of how color, simple images, and similar font, clearly shows a brand. Using the color strip at the bottom also helps readers to identify the genre.

I want to add one final thought on book covers. I know finding quality covers that fit your criteria can be time-consuming, frustrating, and costly. No matter what, find a unique cover. There are a handful of cover models, in a handful of poses, which are rampant on book covers. Try to avoid them at all costs. Personally, I tend to skip right over them because I've seen them so often. They get lost among all the others because they aren't unique and eye-catching. There have been discussions recently on several authors' pages on this topic and the consensus has been that most people are tired of seeing the same covers everywhere.

Having a strong brand will help increase your fan base and your sales.

> *"Create consistent branding between books in a series to make purchasing decisions easy for readers. A unified cover and title style often helps readers recognize connected titles and encourages them to purchase subsequent books."*
> Insights at BookBub.com

Blurb: After your cover, the next important factor is the blurb for your book. Do not get this confused with a synopsis, which has a lot more detail and information. Although not strictly part of branding, your followers will come to expect a similar style pitch, whether humorous, sexy or straightforward.

A Blurb is a few paragraphs that will hopefully entice a reader to either buy the book or to investigate further by downloading a sample. I have to admit I'm not very good at blurbs, but I am getting better.

Have a look at some blurbs for your favorite books on AZ. You could pick up a few tips from their styles.

There are a few books out there offering help, and you could buy a 'blurb' writing service from **Fiverr.com,** but nobody knows your book as well as you do. Not even your editor, who was focused on the writing, not the story.

You need a catchy tag-line/catchphrase, and then a quick introduction to the main characters and story. Include some questions that will require reading the book to find the answers. Never give away the ending, and do not make the questions obvious. For example, if you are writing a romance, which is a 'Happily Ever After' (HEA) genre, there is no point in asking the question, will Jessie end up with Jake? If they are the main characters then, yes, she will. A better question would be "With Jake and John both making her heart beat fast and toying with her affections, how will Jessie ever be able to make up her mind?" This gives the reader a reason to buy the book.

Write a few, and then ask for second opinions, or better yet, post them on your FB page and interact with friends and followers, asking them which they prefer, or ideas for improvement. Never be afraid to ask for help.

If a reader likes your work, they will happily look for more books from you. Which brings me easily to the next point.

You want your readers to become active fans/followers of you and your books. Obviously, readers become fans if they enjoy your books and want to read more. Your goal is moving them from fans to active fans/followers who will share your books with friends and family, as well as across SM.

Interaction is the key to getting active followers. They want to be involved and to be helpful, so asking for their opinion is a good way for you to start building your confidence as well as a fan base.

With a fantastic story, an attractive cover, and an appealing blurb, you are half way there to getting sales. But what is even better for attracting sales? Having an award-winning logo, or a bestselling status. If you have it, flaunt it, as they say! More on that in section 7

.

Categories and Keywords

If you are an indie author, you will have control over your book at publication. You get to choose the categories and keywords for each book. The benefit of being an indie is that you can choose which ones suit your books and change them when you like.

Keywords are an essential part of driving traffic to your book when readers are searching for their next read. There is software available to help you find the best keywords and there are paid services as well. If you have the money and not the time, I would suggest investing in one or the other for keywords and **SEO** support for your website, if you have one.

For keywords, I have, in the past, used [Kindle Samurai](), which cost about $30 to purchase. It did take a little time to work out how to use it. There is now a new app on the market, which does cost more, but has better feedback and reviews, this is [KDP Rocket](). It does cost a lot more at $100, but it may be worth it in the long run. I have never used it, so cannot recommend it, but in the long run, it would be cheaper than hiring someone for each book.

Maybe a few authors could get together and share the expense and help each other? I don't know how it works, but that may be a good idea. If anyone has a copy, maybe you could share your thoughts with me: Allyson.Abbott@hotmail.com

Once you have found a good set of keywords then use them in your blurb as well. If possible using keywords as a subtitle of your book can help as well. A good example of this is taken from my friend Tamara Ferguson. Her first romance book was about a soldier who was wounded and returned home. She discovered that the term 'wounded warrior' was a keyword that was searched for but did not have an extremely large following. This ensured that the term was actually more valuable because only people specifically interested in 'wounded warriors' would search for it. If she had used the term 'injured soldiers' or 'forces romance', there would be far more books available in those categories, so a lot more competition. Having identified that 'wounded warriors' was a good keyword, she then went on to use it as a subtitle, linking it to romance, 'Two Hearts: Wounded Warrior Series' She used the phrase in the book blurb as well. Therefore, her books will show up at the top of any lists whenever anyone searches for that keyword. Since she used the term three times (keywords, subtitle, and blurb), her book is an extremely suitable match for that keyword search. This is all information you can use for your next book if you have missed out on the current one.

As well as the keywords, categories play an important part. Categories include the genre, sub-genre, and any details such as keywords. If you don't mind leaving your ethical hat in the closet for a while, you could slip your fiction story about a dog loving, billionaire hunk, into the non-fiction, dog training category, or possibly 'keep fit'. There are no rules against it on Amazon, if there were, you wouldn't be able to do it. By slotting your book into a category with less competition and fewer books, you will get a higher rank, and that helps with visibility, and therefore sales.

Not everyone likes to do it, and I can appreciate the reasoning, but it's allowed, so why not.

At least you could try it for a week or two to see if it makes any difference and if you are comfortable with the results.

Well, that should keep you busy for a while!

Allyson R. Abbott & Donna Wolz

Section 3: Tools and Techniques

Finding the right tool for the job

There are a lot of tools to help authors with book promotion, marketing, and administration tasks. Some you will have to create yourself, like **ARC Teams** or **Street Teams**. Others are available to tap into, like **BookFunnel**, **MailChimp**, **Rafflecopter** and tools available through Google, or maybe just little tools on your PC to help make life easier. In fact, there are so many it would be impossible to mention everything, but we will help by pointing out a few that we found the most helpful.

Document Management in the 'Cloud'

Being able to share folders and documents over the World Wide Web has got to be one of the most useful tools for work collaboration or projects. The 'cloud' can help with keeping documents safe as well as with sharing. I back up all my work to the cloud, as well as a hard drive. This means I can access my work from anywhere, and if my laptop dies or gets stolen, I still have my work. I cannot imagine how many tears I would cry if I lost all my work. I know a few people who say, 'I can't get on with the cloud, I don't understand it', but they use email. Emails are not stored on your PC, they are in the cloud, you can't access them until you log onto the cloud they are in.

That most people have embraced emails, but still are wary of placing their other files in the cloud, seems odd to me. The cloud is also a great place to store images, as they do tend to take up a lot of storage on a PC, so popping them up there is so much easier. Depending on which cloud you use and how much space you use, will determine the cost. Most clouds offer free storage up to a set amount. I haven't paid for any yet. If I find my free space allowance is running out, I will open another account with another email and store old bits and pieces in there. Most email providers offer some cloud storage for free and usually try to encourage you to use that when sending files, rather than attaching them.

Google

If you don't have a Google account, it is a good idea to create one. There are lots of useful items on Google to help keep you organized and make your life easier. By using Google apps, you never have to worry about losing access to your information because everything you do is safely kept in their cloud storage. All of your files can be easily shared, which can be extremely useful. Google doesn't take up space on your device's memory, which is a big plus. Factor in that it is FREE to store up to 15GB and you can understand why using Google is to your benefit.

I had been using Google for years and had no idea all the useful apps that were available to me. I didn't know what that little square of dots in the upper right corner was for. I had clicked on it but nothing looked useful or interesting to me. When I got involved in the indie book community, I learned how useful they were.

There are so many useful apps in Google. I'm going to talk about the ones I feel will be the most helpful for you to use. These are all found in the drop-down menu from the square of dots. I'm not going to discuss any of the ones found by clicking '*Even more from Google*' at the bottom but I suggest checking out everything Google has to offer because other apps may suit you better than the ones I find most useful.

Google Drive

Drive allows you to upload files and pictures to either save or share. This makes it convenient by keeping everything in one place. You can access your files from any computer.

It is easy to get started with Drive:

To upload a file, simply click on the '*New'* button on the top left of your screen. Choose whether you want to create a new folder or upload a file or folder. It also offers you the option of uploading from a Google app like Forms.

How to Navigate the Social Media Maze

To share with others, highlight the file.

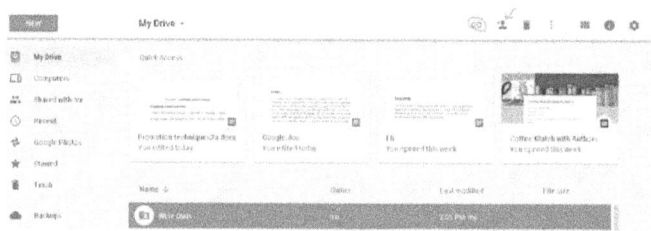

In the upper right corner is an icon for a hyperlink (circled). Click it. The link to share appears. You can choose to let people view, comment, or edit the file by clicking on Sharing Settings.

If you click on the icon of a person (arrow), simply type the name or email address of the person or persons you want to share the file with. Choose whether they can edit or only view the file.

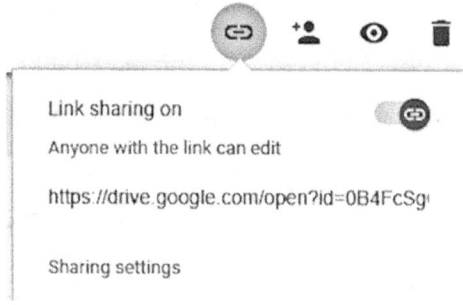

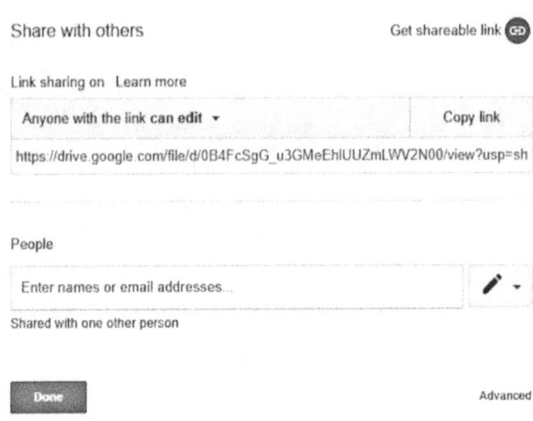

Why would you want to share a file? You may want someone to read what you have written to determine if it makes sense or needs more details. You can share with your beta readers this way. There are many reasons to share files.

Allyson and I used Google Drive to write this book. It allowed us to easily share, edit, add pictures, keep things organized, and everything else we needed to do. Since she is in Spain and I'm in the US, it would have been extremely hard to do all these things without an easy to use, shareable program like this.

We were able to make a copy of what the other had written, then add or remove what needed to be changed, and edit. Plus, since we had made a copies, we could always go back to the original and discuss the changes until we finally agreed on a finished product.

Calendars

Google offers many different types of calendars to meet any need. You can easily switch between the different types of calendars. They are also easy to share. Google calendars can be synced with your phone, other computers, and tablets.

Google Documents, Sheets, Slides, and Forms

Google Documents, Sheets, Slides, and Forms allow you to create so many projects. They are all easily shared. These are very useful if you don't have the software to create these items on your PC.

Google Documents: allows you to create documents with the templates provided. We used Documents in Drive when writing this book.

Google Sheets: allows you to easily create spreadsheets, to-do lists, budgets, expense reports, and calendars.

Google Slides: Slides let you easily create presentations similar to a slide-show, which you could use as a simple trailer. Templates are provided to give you some guidance. If you spend a little time playing around with Slides, you can create a slide-show highlighting a book, series, or all your books. It is so simple to rearrange your slides, add new slides, and edit. This is an alternative to paying someone for a trailer if you are on a tight budget. The only issue I have with Google Slides is that there is no way to attach music to the presentation.

Here is the link to a presentation I made highlighting this book: [Maze Slideshow](#)

Google Forms: are extremely useful. I use forms all the time. You can create an entry form or a quiz for a contest. Create a sign-up form for ARCs or Review links or whatever you need. The possibilities are endless.

How to Navigate the Social Media Maze

There are a variety of templates available. I find the blank form to be all I ever need. With a blank form, you can add a title and description, add pictures and video, add more sections, and ask questions. The responses to the questions can be short answer, paragraph, multiple choice, checkboxes, or drop-down menu. You can make a question/answer required or not. Responses can be viewed as a spreadsheet or each response can be viewed individually.

From Allyson: Before reading Donna's tip below, I would like to mention that I struggled to find the 'Form' app. It did not show up on my Google Docs page, nor was it offered as a 'new' doc to create. I did, however, find it on my Google Drive page, under 'New', top left of the page, and under the options of Google Docs, Sheets and Slides, it says More…, when you click on this you find Forms, Drawings, My Maps and Sites, so even more to explore!

Tip: Creating a Google Form:

When you open a new Form, this screen appears:

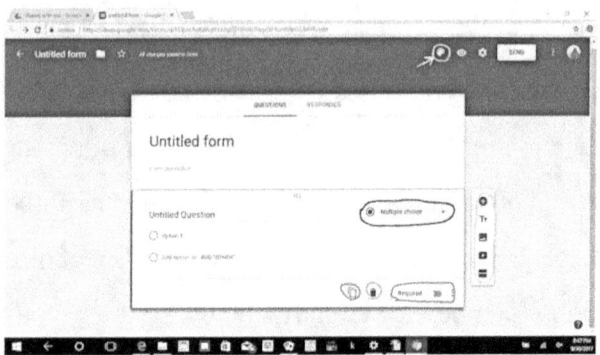

Click on Untitled Form and add a title. Then add a description. Now you are ready to add questions to the Form.

In the section circled in yellow (vertical column) are the buttons you will use to make a Form. The top button allows you to add a question, followed by add title and description. Next is the add image button, followed by add video, and last is add section. You can do these steps in any order.

Circled in blue (top circle) is the drop-down menu to choose the type of question. In gr een (bottom right)is where you make it a required question, pink (bottom left) is to make a duplicate of the question, and purple (bottom middle) is to delete the question. Everything is conveniently located for you to use.

If you click on the Settings icon, you can choose to collect email addresses, allow the respondents to edit their responses or submit another response, and several other options.

If you click the Color Palette, circled in white, you can change the background color. You can also add a picture to the top of the form. This is a good way to personalize the form with your logo or an image of your book.

Once the form is complete, you are ready to share it.

Press the Send button in the upper right-hand corner

The followings screen will appear

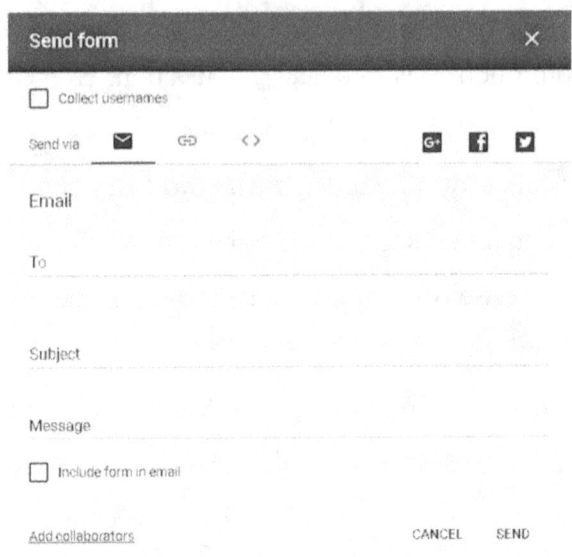

You can now email the link. This is useful if you want to share the link with one or two people. In the bottom left-hand corner it says 'Add collaborators.' This allows you to designate certain people who can edit what you share.

Click the hyperlink symbol (to the right of the email symbol) and this screen appears:

How to Navigate the Social Media Maze

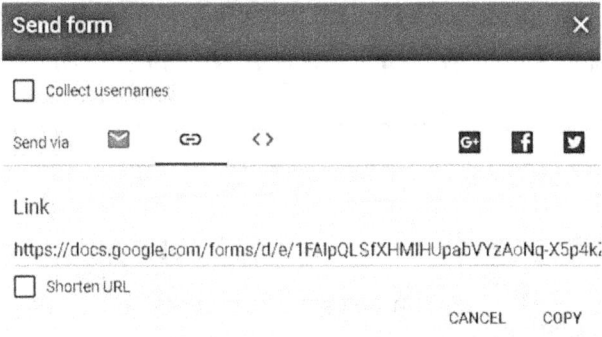

You can now copy the URL and share it anywhere. This is also convenient because you can shorten the URL to a more manageable length by checking the box.

If you click on <>, a link will appear giving you an Embedded HTML link to use.

To share on G+, Facebook, or Twitter, simply click on the appropriate icon. So easy.

Blogger

Blogger allows you to create a blog for free. You don't need to pay anyone to set it up for you because it is super easy. Play around with Blogger and learn all it can do. Keep track of what you want to incorporate into your site and then create it. You can always change things as you discover what works for you and what doesn't. So don't freak out at the thought of setting it up. Take your time and you will have it ready before you know it.

Even if you don't want to set up a blog, play around with it. Blogger can be useful if you plan on contacting blogs about posting your book information, most of them will want the information in HTML (Hyper Text Markup Language), which makes it easier to post information. You can convert plain text to HTML and vice-versa with ease on Blogger.

How to Navigate the Social Media Maze

Tip: Create the post you want the blogs to share, including pictures, on Blogger. Click on the HTML tab in the upper left corner and it is converted. If you then copy and paste it onto a blank document and send it to the bloggers, they will only have to copy and paste and everyone who blogs will have the same layout and the same structure, which helps with your branding and image. This is what blog tour promoters do. This only works for blogs though. If the blogger is using FB they will still need the word docs and the images to post. (*more on blogs later*).

Google Keep

Keep lets you save your thoughts as notes, lists, and voice memos from anywhere. This can be useful when an idea pops into your head at an inconvenient time, but you know it is perfect for the book you are writing, or a future book. There are a few more note-taking apps mentioned later.

As I mentioned earlier, these are the Google apps I find most useful. Google has dozens more apps available, so take a look at all Google has to offer.

There are of course other tools you can use that do not belong to Google.

Sticky Notes

I am a 'list maker' and 'keeper of notes and bits of paper', but the problem is I can never find them when I want them. A few years ago I discovered an app that I could download on my laptop, which was basically 'E-Post it' notes for your PC screen. You could create them and have them placed anywhere on the screen to keep information visible, long or short term. Recently, I found that Microsoft has a very similar app called Sticky Notes. You can find it in the list of all the programs and apps on your PC. I find it extremely useful, especially if I just want a holding place for a web link, a bit of information I have just copied, or a list of jobs I need to do that day, week, or month. You can allocate different colors to the sticky notes, so I have green for personal and yellow for book tasks.

You can have them visible all the time on your desktop, or turn them off when you don't need them. The app is free, so I am sharing this information because I find it very useful.

Two other apps that I find useful are OneNote and the Calendar. OneNote is great for sharing information if you are working on a project with someone, and the calendar speaks for itself. They are both easy to use and there is always the 'help' button to find out more information.

Evernote

Evernote is a program that comes highly recommended and can be downloaded if you prefer it. You can collect all your notes together in one place, even handwritten notes. It is quite useful if you are working on a team. It has templates for creative writing, as well as tools to help you achieve your targets. If you wanted to write so many words a day by the end of the week, you could set up your goal and the chart will show your progress, or you can use it as a checklist for jobs done and even for dictation.

Helpful links

[PC Mag Evernote Review](#)
[Evernote v OneNote](#)
[Evernote user reviews](#)

Again, I would suggest doing a little research first, although I do know of some authors who use this to organize their life. However, the last thing you need are more apps to clutter up your desktop and your time, if you don't use them. I like to be organized, but I am a list making person; usually with pen and paper, and notes on my on-screen post its. Everyone has their own system and you will find yours.

Dropbox

If you don't have a Google account there are other apps available. Dropbox is one of the most popular and well known 'cloud' sharing platforms. It works on the same basis as Google Drive, where you can upload files and documents to folders in the 'cloud' and share access to them with other people. You can choose which folders or documents you share. I (Allyson) use Dropbox a lot, especially when I am on the road, without the constant use of a laptop or the internet. I know that sounds strange, but I have very often handwritten my books, mostly due to lack of electricity, to keep the laptop charged. Or maybe we only traveled with one laptop between me and my husband. I found it easy to use a notebook to write in, but I am not a very good typist and couldn't face typing up pages of written work. I did try the dictation software once, but that made so much extra work and editing, I gave it up as a bad idea.

Anyway, my final solution was to use an app on my iPhone 'Tiny Scanner', to scan the documents and when we found a coffee shop or store that had free Wi-Fi, I would upload the scanned documents to my Dropbox (the process was made easy through the app), and put them in a folder I shared with Christine, a lovely lady from Austin, Texas, who I found through Fiverr.com. She would then type up my handwritten notes and pop them back into the Dropbox when completed. The system works great.

Right, so now you have had a sample of a few tools you can use. Let's move on to SM, and how you can implement what is available to help promote your books.

Section 4:
Social Media

Suddenly launching yourself into the world of indie authors on Social Media can be intimidating. As a serious author--- and I mean serious about being an author and not writing about serious things---you need to take a deep breath, say three times while spinning in a circle, I believe in myself, I believe in myself, I believe in myself, and then jump right in.

Have faith when I tell you, you are not the only one who has the jitters about opening yourself up to the world as an author. I think everyone also stared wide-eyed at the headlights for a while. But once you write a few posts, interact with other writers and join in with events, it will soon get easier. When you first interact or write a tweet or post, nobody knows it is your first one, or your first week.

There are so many SM platforms to join or sign up to, it becomes a bit of a quagmire. Do you sign up for everything, just the major ones, or a few?

My advice would be to start with a few and build up. Do some research about each one before you start, but you will probably want to start with the two largest SM platforms, FB and Twitter.

Social Media tasks can suck so many hours from your day. The more you sign up to and use, the more time it will take, although there are social media management systems available to help with some tasks. We will be discussing those in the next section.

In the SM section, we will be concentrating on how you as an author can use these platforms to help you network and promote your books.

We are looking in depth at FB, Twitter, and G+, then we will discuss Pinterest and LinkedIn options and then we will take a brief look at other options. Please remember that we are concentrating on how authors can use these platforms and we are not explaining all the functions. If you want to learn more about the platforms I suggest you buy books that are new and relevant for the ones you are interested in. We are here to help give you a good starting point

Facebook

Facebook is the #1 SM site. There is a large and active indie book community you should get involved with to help you spread the word about you and your books. If you only use one SM platform, I suggest you make it FB.

When we first got involved in the indie book community on FB, neither of us had any idea how much there was to learn. We had no idea what 'groups' were and how useful they would be, or how plentiful they were. We had no idea what a takeover was, or that you can create as many pages as you want, or that you can boost your posts to hundreds and thousands of people for only a few dollars. There were so many things available and so much to learn.

In this section, I will suggest ways to use FB to your advantage, and hopefully, help you avoid some of the mistakes Allyson and I made, and to get the most out of your experience. Once again, this is general information you can adapt to fit your needs.

How to Navigate the Social Media Maze

One thing to keep in mind is the fact that FB is always changing their rules/policies. They don't publicize these changes. They simply implement the new rules/policies. Be sure you pay attention to FB posts concerning any changes to FB rules/policies. If you're not sure about what is acceptable, check out the [Help Section](#) on FB.

You probably already have profile on FB. That is terrific, because you know how FB works. The information I am offering first is for setting up your Author page. While most things are the same, there are some aspects you will need to do differently.

Creating Your Author Page

When you create your page, choose Artist, Band, or Public Figure. Then from the drop-down menu, choose author. Add your name and click enter.

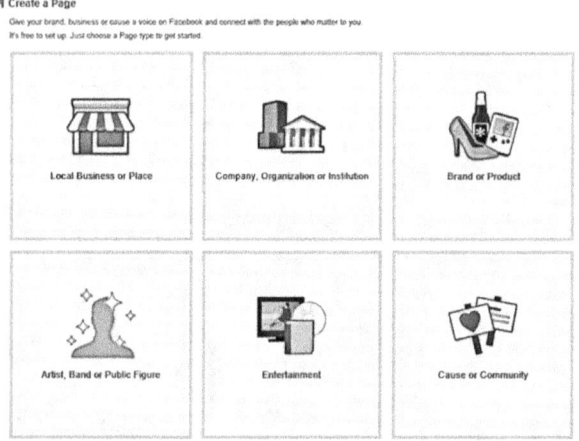

How to Navigate the Social Media Maze

Make sure your account states you are an author. Add it to your name. This is important when readers are trying to find your page or sharing your books. It allows them to know they have found the correct person. I can't emphasize this enough. I tag a lot of authors since I am always promoting. Many times I can't tag them because I don't know which profile to choose from the options offered. It is amazing how many people have the same name and how useless some Profile Pictures turn out to be.

Your **Profile Picture** should be a picture of you or one of your books or your logo. This allows people to better recognize it as your account. Plus, it allows them to associate you with a particular image. This helps with your **branding**. My recommendation is to use the same profile picture on all of your SM accounts.

Set up your page to post Public. If you restrict who can see your posts, you are hurting your chances of being seen. This also allows people to share posts from your page. You want as many people as possible to share your posts. Allow followers to post to your page. This can be a great way to create interaction.

If, or when, you offer things strictly to your followers, you can change the setting of that post so only followers can see it.

In the '**About**' section, list your bio and your social media (**stalker**) links, your books and the buy links. This is a great way to allow people to follow you across SM and buy your books without a hassle.

Your '**Cover Photo**' is another opportunity to promote your work and strengthen your brand. Use your book covers, tag-line, your picture, and/or your logo to create a banner that will provide a lot of information to people who visit your page. This acts as a 'hook' to get visitors to check out the rest of the page.

Okay, you've got your Facebook page ready to go. What now?

How to Get The Most Out Of Using Facebook

Obviously, you are going to promote your books on FB. Before you can do that, you have to build a following. Invite family and friends to like your page. Ask them to share your page and invite their relatives and friends. This will garner a small group of followers to get you started.

By following other authors, pages or groups it will put their posts into your news feed, so the same can be said for people who follow you. Therefore building up followers is an easy way to get your books noticed by more people.

Now you need to figure out the best way to get more followers.

To get more followers, you need to:

- Interact with the followers you already have
- Become active with other authors,
- Get involved in book groups--especially those created for your genre
- Find bloggers who read and review your genre.

Remember, gaining '**likes**' for your page allows more people to see your posts and then hopefully share your posts. You can 'like' other people pages and then you will see their posts. All of this helps to promote each other's work. So basically, the more likes, the more publicity. It is the same with friends. The more friends you have, the more publicity you will get.

Let's look at each one and see what you can do.

To interact with your followers you should promote your books, share the covers, banners, blurb, buy links, and teasers. Share snippets from the book. Hold contests to give away a few copies; either ebook or signed PB. Play a game using information from the book. Anything you can think of to garner attention for the book. Ask your followers to share the book across SM. If the book has not yet been published, you can ask for advice on the cover, or title, or even characters names or places. By getting your followers or potential fans involved right from the start, it encourages ownership and builds a relationship with you and your books.

How to Navigate the Social Media Maze

You also need to interact with your followers on topics other than your books; to me, this is one of the most important aspects of Facebook.

If all you ever do is push your book(s), readers get turned off. It becomes boring. Why look at your page today when they know it will be more of the same as yesterday? Talk about your pets, silly things you've seen or done, your vacation, etc. Post interesting pictures, videos, or articles. Ask your readers their opinions or to share something with you. Promote other authors books. This lets readers connect with you. It also allows them to know you care about them and value them beyond simply buying your books. By doing these things, you are strengthening the fan base you have. If your fan base enjoys interacting with you, they are more apt to tell their friends about you and to share your books across social media platforms; this, in turn, will lead to more people hearing about you and your books.

Another thing that keeps readers/followers interested is to share things exclusively with them. Share tidbits of your work-in-progress. Do a 'cover reveal' before you share it with the general public. Offer bonus scenes or free books. Write a short story just for them, hold a Giveaway for loyal fans; the possibilities are endless. Be creative, be unique, and ask for their suggestions.

Interact with authors, particularly ones who write books similar to yours. It stands to reason, if they write similar books, their readers will be interested in your books as well. Promote their books to your readers. Be sure to **tag** them. After you have been active on their pages for a little while and have shared their books, ask them for permission to mention your book to their readers. I guarantee you will get a positive response from most authors.

Ask authors you have been following to read and review your books. You can contact them directly when your book is nearly ready to publish and ask them if they would like to read it. Authors are also readers and many will be happy to read it. Others might want to read it but don't have time. Some won't be interested at all. Always be gracious to each one, you never know what is going on in their lives at the time.

How to Navigate the Social Media Maze

Help other authors whenever you can. You could offer to read and review for any author willing to help you. However, be careful not to over commit and then not follow through. The indie movement is extremely supportive and you should always add your support when you can.

Get involved with groups. FB has thousands of groups created for the purpose of promoting, discussing or offering services for authors and their books. We have a huge list of groups (nearly 1000) for you to browse through HERE sorted into genres/interests, specifically for promotion, support or discussion. In *How to Navigate the Road to Building Reviews*, there will be another large list of groups that help with reviews.

Find groups that cater to your genre as well as groups that allow all genres to be posted. Just search in the search box for related terms like books, reviews, writers, authors etc. Many readers are like me and read several different genres, so general interest groups are important, too. Some groups have rules concerning price and frequency of posts. It is important you follow the rules.

Always read the description of the group, so you will know what is, and isn't, allowed. If it appears to be a good fit for you and your books, join the group. Join as many groups as possible so you have multiple opportunities to share your book. Warning: Don't join over 20 or so groups in one day. Spread it over time. For some strange reason, FB frowns upon too much joining.

Don't ignore small groups in favor of large groups. Join groups that are a fit for you and your books regardless of size. Just because a group has 20,000 members doesn't guarantee your posts will be seen by a large number of people.

Post to several groups every day. Each day, post in different groups. Post at different times of the day to increase your chances of reaching more people. Again, don't post in too many groups at once because Facebook will put you in their 'time-out chair', or what is known as Facebook jail. How long you are in jail varies. You want to stay out of jail because you can't to authors. Most, but not all, will read and review your book and share with their followers. I'm mentioning them under FB because most book bloggers have an FB page associated with their blog. Find their FB page and find out what genres they read as well as information about the bloggers. In addition to the fantastic share anything until you are free.

Keep a list of your groups. Start at the top and work your way through the list. This allows you to post to all the groups before you start back at the top. You don't want to post to the same few groups over and over because that will limit your reach.

Book bloggers are extremely important list of FB groups mentioned above, we also have a huge list of FB blog pages that will be made available through *How to Navigate the Road to Building Reviews*. The FB pages will help you to access people to help build up your book reviews.

Check through them and if they read your genre, contact them to inquire if they would be interested in reading and reviewing your book. Make your inquiry as friendly as possible and mention why you think they would be a good fit for your book. Mention something you learned about the blog. Tell them if someone recommended them and who that person was. In other words, make your inquiry similar to a letter you would write a friend. You could always mention finding them through this book.

Two important points to keep in mind when contacting anyone to review your book: **NEVER** offer compensation in exchange for a review. **Always** let the reviewer know that all you are asking for is an honest opinion.

Be prepared to send them a media kit so they have all the information needed to share your book. Blogs can only showcase your book if you send them the tools to do so. If they have a Blog (like on WordPress or Blogger) as well, they may ask for an **HTML** code, which is discussed later in the book. Don't panic, we will help. Sometimes it helps to do a Giveaway if you have a blog posting about your book. This can help if you require entrants to like your page or follow you on other SM sites to enter the giveaway.

So, now you are growing your fan base but you still need to increase your promotional reach. How do you do that without spending a lot of money? You don't have to do it alone. Create a Street Team.

As we (Allyson and Donna) have different experiences and knowledge from our approaches to promotion, we have different ideas of Street Teams.

Street Teams (Allyson's point of view)

A street team is a team of readers/fans/family members who an author calls upon to help out with tasks such as promoting, reviewing, posting information, looking after emails, social media and anything else an author is happy to pass on to someone else to do.

I was very hesitant and not at all comfortable about presuming that just because someone had read one of my books they could now be called a 'fan'. So actually reaching out to my readers was harder than approaching a total stranger. At the end of ebooks you tend to get the option to review the book, so if a reader had not done that, there may be a reason.

I don't think it is until you have built up sales and reviews, and started a relationship with readers, especially if you are a new author and new to promoting, that you can begin to relax a bit and ask openly for reviews. This is just my opinion. Or maybe I was just lacking in confidence!

But, back to Street Teams. Street team members work for free. They do it for the love of working with and helping an author. The author appreciates their time and value and may even reward them with free books, swag or even a gift card or two. Some authors also run giveaways and bonus schemes for their teams, to encourage loyalty and to thank them in an official way.

In practice, having an ST gives the author more time to concentrate on their writing. If the team is fairly large they will also appoint someone as head of the team to look after the members. They could also have several small teams who specialize in specific tasks. For example, a beta reading team may be good at reading and giving feedback, but hopeless at promotion techniques.

Getting a street team is the hardest part. If you have a PA, you could include it as part of their job, to enroll street team members. You could ask family, and then extend it to friends, and then their friends.

I have a small team that I managed to build when I needed some reviews for a book; more on this in How to Navigate the Road to Building Reviews. To keep and build a team you really need to send out regular emails and requests for small tasks or jobs, this will retain their interest and make them feel their part in your career is valuable, which it is! Any help you can get is always valuable. If you find one person in the team is more hands-on than the others, you could see if that person is willing to take on more responsibility and manage the team for you, thus you'll only have one main contact to deal with, therefore cutting down on your work so you can concentrate on your writing.

Promoting your book is going to take a lot of time, so it may be worth trying to build a team, from the beginning, even before your book is written. You could start with family and friends and then add other people as they come along. They could help with the SM platform building, posting for you on Twitter or FB, writing your blog posts, helping develop your story with ideas or feedback. The earlier you start, the better your team will be. I very often would send my rough stories to a friend for her opinion, this was beta reading and very helpful.

Helpful links

What-is-a-street-team?
6 steps to Build a Street Team
One author's approach to assembling a Street Team

A lot of authors now try to have a 'team' specifically for review writing. You could call this your ARC or Review team, but they could also be a part of the main street team. Just because one of your team members is an ace on Twitter, and keeps your posts up to date, does not mean they can't review your book. On the other hand, you may have someone helping you who is really arty and produces beautiful banners but dislikes writing reviews. Would you exclude them from your team? No, you wouldn't. Anyone who is willing to help, you would gratefully accept the offer.

One of the most potent tools in an author's armor is having a lot of reviews for your book upon publication, so you need to try and build a team of trustworthy readers, who will read your ARC in advance of publication, and then post the review before or as soon as it is live. The more reliable the team, the more reviews you may get. This, in turn, leads to you getting more publicity from AZ, especially if sales are pouring in through all your promotional work.

Donna will go into detail on ARC Teams in our next book *How to Navigate the Road to Building Reviews*.

Street Teams (Donna's Tips)

Street Teams are a group of your fans who promote your work on a regular basis across all of SM. This doesn't have to be a large group. Just a few people can easily help you expand your reach. You want a ST with active members you can count on.

Street Teams can be found on SM platforms other than FB. However, they are most common on Facebook. If you want to create a ST on another platform, the same basic steps and rules apply.

You typically have a separate FB page for your ST. Give the group a unique name that goes along with the type of books you write, is something relevant to you, or just a catchy name.

Before you create your ST Facebook page, type the name you have chosen into the FB Search Bar. This will show you if the name is already being used or if there is a similar name in use. For example, I'm a member of two Street Teams with the word Angels in the name. There are several other Street Teams using

Angels. So, it would be best to avoid using Angels in your name.

To recruit members to your ST, ask your followers if they would be interested in being part of the team. When you send a newsletter, let them know you are forming a team and how to join. Tweet about forming a team. Post the information in your posts when promoting your books. Once again, be creative.

When you are recruiting, be sure to let them know exactly what you expect from them. For example, you could create a post every morning and post it to the Team page. You expect them to share these posts with five groups a minimum of three times a week. That means you are asking them to invest 5-10 minutes a week promoting you. Or you will make posts they can share and ask them to promote whenever they can. It is up to you.

Typically, ST members are eligible for exclusive Giveaways, **Sneak Peeks**, **ficlets**, whatever you decide.

My suggestion is to make Giveaways open only to active members. People may join your ST just to get the extras and NEVER promote you in any way. You want to give people a reason to promote you. Whether or not you offer regular Giveaways is up to you. However, offering them something in return for the free advertising they do, seems only fair to me and many other like-minded readers.

Just recently, several authors whose Street Teams I am a member of, took their active members and formed a new secret group. In one case the author had over 1100 members on her ST. Only 30 were active. Now, she shares more private information with us and asks our opinions more often. She knows we have her back and is rewarding us by doing these things.

Several ways to check participation: If they tag you like they should, you will get notified of every share and you can keep track of them. This is time-consuming on your part. You could designate a post on the street team page for them to post their links, it would need to be the pinned post so it is easy to find. This way is easier for you and the members, but it means you can't have a pinned post for anything else.

My suggestion is to have them put the link to each of their shares on a Google Form. Each link is one entry into a Giveaway for the month. Personally, I prefer the Google Form option, because it is the easiest way to keep up with who shared as well as where they shared.

I urge you to remove people from your Team who never promote you. They belong on your Author page, not your ST.

It is quite common to have someone help you with the ST page. They can keep up with shares, post messages to share and reminders for other members, or anything else you decide on. You still need to be active on the page and interact with members.

Facebook Promotional Activities

There are different types of promotional activities on FB. All of them are terrific ways to get noticed by more people. I'm going to briefly touch on them here. More details are provided in Section 7: Promotion Methods.

Blog Tours: These are typically run by a **PR group** but you can run one yourself. Blogs are contacted and asked to promote your book on their blog.

Cover Reveal / Book Release: Usually a one-day event where blogs promote your cover reveal, or release day.

FB Event/Party: These can be held on your author page, on an event page you create, or with the help of a PR group or FB group. How long they last depends on what you plan to do during the event/party.

Take Over: A Take Over is when an author is scheduled to chat with readers on another author's page, or in an FB group, or during another author's event/party, etc.

How to Navigate the Social Media Maze

FB Hop: A Hop involves numerous people/groups getting together to give away prizes across different pages.

Take-over your own page: You can be 'live' on your author or street team page. Some authors are doing live video feeds as well.

FB Ads: 2017 has seen big changes in the way you can use FB to create advertising for your books. They can be created under the Create Ad listing.

FB Post boosts: Are surprisingly cheap and easy to do. This can be a quick easy way to expand your reach without breaking your budget.

Bookbots Bob and Bill

Bookbot Bob is a new app available to use with Facebook. It sends your book information to their followers on a certain date via a personal message known as a PM. Readers simply sign up for the service choosing the genres they wish to read. They are contacted via Messenger on Facebook.

Here is a copy of their sign-up form for a one-day promotion. The cost is $10. They also offer a week-long promo for $15.

Bookbot Bob Booking Form
Please complete the form to submit your book. Make sure your book meets the requirements before submitting. These are:

Minimum 10 reviews, average 4*. (If it's a new release with no reviews, please provide links to your other books with good reviews. I may waive this requirement in that case.)

FULL-LENGTH BOOKS ONLY.

No multi-author box sets.

The same book or author may only be featured ONCE every 12 weeks to keep the content fresh for the readers.

ABSOLUTELY NO BOOKS THAT REQUIRE A READER SIGN UP TO A LIST

ONE CATEGORY PER BOOK ONLY

Please choose: *
- ◉ $10 (due at time of booking)
- ○ I'm on the VIP list
- ○ IndieGoGo Supporter (please make sure your name is the same as it appears on your campaign contribution)

Booking Form - Welcome Book Promo - PLEASE READ
Please complete the form to submit your book. Make sure your book meets the requirements before submitting. These are:

Minimum 10 reviews, average 4*. (If it's a new release with no reviews, please provide links to your other books with good reviews. I may waive this requirement in that case.)

Full-length books only.

Free.

No multi-author boxed sets.

Must be available on all major platforms.

The same book can be featured more than once for this promo as this is the first book readers will see (no duplication). However, to keep the content fresh for readers, if you book a Welcome Promo you won't be able to book a standard promo for 24 weeks to keep the content fresh for the readers.

ABSOLUTELY NO BOOKS THAT REQUIRE A READER SIGN UP TO A LIST

IF YOU WANT TO BOOK MORE THAN ONE GENRE, PLEASE SUBMIT A NEW FORM FOR EACH GENRE

How to Navigate the Social Media Maze

Bob is for free books and Bill is for discounted books. Your book will be the only one offered in your genre on the date you choose. You might want to try this as a way to get your book seen by more people. Remember, offering your book for free is a good way to make more people aware of your work. This means you have a better chance at getting reviews and future sales of your other books.

There is so much going on in the book community on FB. Authors and readers are always coming up with new ideas and concepts. Keep your eyes and ears open to all the information available to you. Pick what you feel comfortable using, adapt it to your specific needs, and never give up. Reach out to others for help. There are many, many people who are willing to offer advice and help if you simply ask.

Twitter

When I first started writing I hesitated to open a Twitter account. I knew I needed to have a social media presence, but it was all very scary. Twitter looked fast-paced, with a weird shorthand language, and the hashtags looked like a secret code, and in a way they are.

Twitter is the second most used SM platform in the indie book community. Apart from FB, I would suggest that Twitter is going to be your next best friend. It is for me, anyway.

I only know a few authors who do not embrace Twitter, and if they do not want to spend a lot of time promoting or chatting with followers, I don't blame them. I do think it's important to have a plan for SM use, as mentioned by Donna in Section 2. If you only want to spend an hour a day answering emails, posting on a blog, updating your website, then Twitter is not for you. Twitter does need a little time to cultivate a following and to gain trust.

How to Navigate the Social Media Maze

I spend a lot less time on Twitter than I did a few months ago, but this is only because I now schedule my tweets through a scheduling program called **Twittimer** and I use **Crowdfire.com** to manage followers and who I'm following (more on these in section 6).

Before Twittimer and Crowdfire, I would log onto my account and follow a few people, authors, reviewers and bloggers, etc. and re-tweet one, or a few posts. It would take up about half an hour to an hour if I also posted a few tweets about my books. It's important to remember, the more books you have the more promotion is involved.

Creating a profile

Let's start at the beginning. You need to register and open an account and create a profile name. They also ask for a password and a second security checking system, this may be an **SMS** or email. That is very easy to do.

You will need to create a handle. Your handle is a shortened version of your name with an 'at' symbol @ in front, so my handle is @AllysonRAbbott. You will be given a few options to choose from or you can make your own, but if someone else has already claimed it, you can't use it. A lot of authors use the word 'author' in their name and handle, and actually, this is a good idea. It confirms who you are and it helps with visibility if other users are searching for authors. Some authors use 'athr' to show they are an author, which saves two letters over the complete word. Also, consider using only an initial for your first name if that will allow you to use the word author. The problem is you only have 15 characters to create a handle, so choose wisely.

You can have more than one account, but each account needs a new email address.

You can add a picture, and I would suggest using the same one you use for Facebook, your Amazon Author page, your blog site and website and any other social media platforms. Your image is part of your branding, so you need to be recognized straight-away. Don't make it hard for your fans to find you.

You can also have a banner, which can be the same as your FB banner but wouldn't you know---it's a different size. So you may need to shrink the FB banner to fit or probably resize it in a graphics program to fit perfectly.

The following link tells you the sizes of the different banners required for different social media. I would love to say keep it handy, but they are always altering their sizes. So make sure you check the requirements before creating the banner. I have no idea why, but I am always having problems with the Twitter banner. It never seems to fit properly, even though I follow instructions carefully. Therefore, I suggest the simpler the better, or follow Donna's advice and make it a bit smaller than the dimensions they give.

Helpful link

Social Media Image sizes 2017

You also have 160 characters to write a short bio or to introduce yourself. Use abbreviations to save characters. Make it meaningful, and if you haven't put 'author' in your handle/username, then I suggest you write it in there. You can mention your genre, or if you are published, but make it short, sharp, chatty, and informative. Make it amusing or unique, if you can. It is a challenge with only 160 characters.

This link will take you to a [Twitter support page](#) offering advice on how to open an account.

During the sign-up process, they also ask you a few questions to determine what you would like in your feed. Make them appropriate to you and your books.

Once you get signed up you will be able to see your page. In the top right-hand corner is the search bar, so first off search for authors, or aspiring authors or romance, or whatever is appropriate. Find a few authors and follow their profiles by opening their profile page and clicking on the 'follow' button. It is also a good idea to follow some blogs and reader groups.

How to Navigate the Social Media Maze

On your homepage, you will see these four tabs across the top: Home, Moments, Notification and Message. By the search bar is your profile picture and a Tweet button. If you click on your profile picture you will get a drop-down list with links to edit your profile, change and view lists and interact with your page analytics and settings.

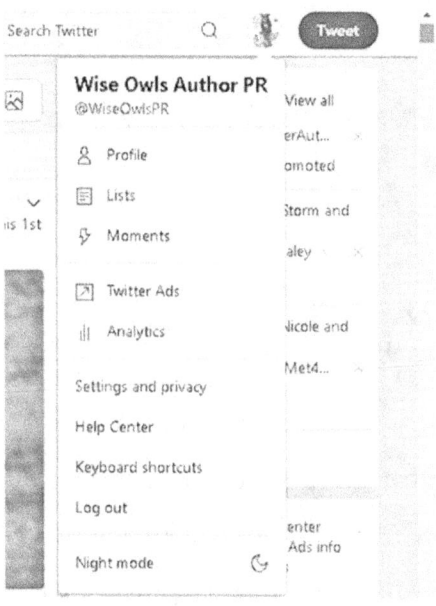

If you click the Moments tab, it will take you to a list of curated stories covering the current, popular topics that are relevant to you, based on your location and who you follow. Here is a link to learn more about Moments: Creating a moment on Twitter.

The Notifications tab will show you who has liked your tweets, followed you, retweeted your tweets, or added you to a list. This makes it easy to see who is interacting with your account.

The Messages tab shows who you have messaged and who has sent you messages.

Now, let's take a closer look at your Homepage.

Your homepage is made up of three columns:

Far left column:

To the left is a miniature profile picture and banner, and under that is a record of how many tweets you have made, how many you are following and how many followers you have. You can click on any of those three numbers and it will take you to a page to see more details.

I sometimes use the 'followers' link to see who is following me that I can follow back. I don't follow everyone, because some are scammers with fake profiles and, to be honest, some are just plain creepy. Being a writer of romance and erotica, I have my fair share of 'come-ons', so I tend to avoid the ones that do not appear to be romance fans. My difficulty is that I write non-fiction as well and these books are written for anyone. However, using the 'followers' link is a good way to begin building up your numbers.

If you click on Tweets under your miniature profile picture it will take you to your tweets stream. Under the banner, you will see tabs that say 'likes, lists, and moments'. The likes are how many people have liked your tweets, the lists are the ones you have made (more on that later), and moments are those you have created.

Below that is a list of **'trends'.** You can decide if you want the random trends chosen by Twitter, or you can have them linked to a country or theme. I have mine set to the USA, but it is easy to change.

Middle column:

The middle column is made up of the tweets from people you follow, with a space at the top you can tweet from. At the bottom of each tweet are options to make a comment, to retweet, to like (click on the heart) or to send a direct message.

For speed, liking and retweeting will serve you well, especially if you are writing something as you retweet. Users love having their posts retweeted and you may be rewarded by a 'follow' or a retweet of one of your tweets later on down the road.

Right-hand column:

The right-hand column generally has sponsored posts or suggestions for follows.

So that, basically, is your Twitter page. The more people you follow, the more the feeds will change. On your homepage, it shows a number at the top of how many 'new tweets' have happened since you logged on. You will need to refresh the page to update it. The more people you follow the more tweets you will get.

How to Navigate the Social Media Maze

With apps like Crowdfire.com that link to your Twitter account, you can quickly see who follows, who you follow and who doesn't follow you back, etc. It really does help. Stay busy on Twitter, even if you only drop in once or twice a week, you need to keep active and build a following and network with others when you can. My sales have improved since tweeting and retweeting others. A lot of people will reciprocate. Nobody is ever going to say 'hey, you can't retweet that!" Most tweeters will be happy that someone is taking an interest in their tweets. You need to build up followers, to do that you need to follow others, and to do that you need to be seen as active. There is a lot to learn on Twitter that can help you connect with other authors or readers.

Okay, I can hear you saying, but how does this help me?

Once I came to grips with my wariness of using Twitter and I took advice from a friend, I have never looked back. The first advice I read about Twitter was that you need to interact, to build trust, to make friends, to contact and thank your followers. I did try all this, and

I discovered that even though I poked my nose into conversations or sent messages, the majority were ignored, sending me scurrying back to my insecurity cave. However, my friend advised me to build followers (mainly from authors and book lovers) and tweet about my books. Having nothing to lose, I did. I am happy to report that my book sales increased. I now have quite a few followers and follow over 6k. This is not a lot from seeing other profiles, but I keep adding, and the retweets and follows keep happening.

Allyson R. Abbott
@AllysonRAbbott

Tweets 11.9K
Following 6,497
Followers 7,335

Most of this action keeps my picture and name in front of readers. Hopefully, they will remember me and buy a book in the future.

How to Navigate the Social Media Maze

As this book is aimed towards new Twitter users and how to get the best out of Twitter for promoting you and your books, I am going to try and keep it all simple. I will place links at the end of this section in case you want to develop it more or use more of the tools available.

How to build A Following from scratch

I have mentioned I like to be organized, so I tend to use a spreadsheet to monitor which tweets I send out each day. This is because you cannot send out the same tweet within 24hrs. You can reword it, or add a few different words and use the same image, but never just a direct repeat or retweet. Each tweet is made up of 140 characters plus an image and you can tag people as well.

As a new Twitter user and an author, I think that by understanding the following elements and tools you will have enough to keep you busy, gain followers and find relevant people to follow.

Lists: The first tool that you need to use is the 'list' option.

I suggest to get some follows and followers, you need to find authors whom you respect, follow on AZ or Bookbub, or who write in the same genre as you; preferably those who have a large following themselves. You can follow who you like, if they don't like it, they can block you, but generally, everyone likes to be followed. Once you have are comfortable tweeting and retweeting it is time to build your numbers. Twitter does have limits on how many people you can follow or unfollow in one day. As a newbie, you need to follow, but not aggressively; so a couple hundred a day, rather than two thousand, will be allowed and it's easy to do.

As you read through the tweets on your homepage feed, click on their picture to go to their profile. Under their banner check the tabs and see if there is the word 'list' and if there are any numbers underneath. If there is a number then click on it. It will show you a page with a list of lists that the user has created. Each list will have a name and the number of members in the list and the name of the person who actually created the list. The person who creates the original list may not necessarily be the person who has the list at the moment. Anyone can subscribe to a list, which is what you are going to do.

Have a look at the names of the lists and see if there are any with a few hundred or thousand members. If they are linked to authors or books, then click on the list, and then on the left, click subscribe. It will show you how many other people subscribe.

Once you subscribe, the list will now be attached to your profile, giving you easy access to lists of authors or book lovers. I have about ninety-six lists, so you can always pop over to my profile, @AllysonRAbbott. Every day, go to a list and follow about two-hundred of them. Some will follow you back, some won't but don't worry about that yet. What you need is to link your account with other authors. Authors share and help, so if you retweet their tweets, then they may retweet yours. If they have thousands of followers your book and profile become more visible.

Follows and Following: You also need to keep in touch with who is following you. On a regular basis, you need to go to your page and click on your 'Followers' number, to see who has started following you, and just scroll down to see if you are following your followers. It is not necessarily good to follow all those who follow you because there are some unscrupulous people who could be scammers, so read their profiles and decide. You can always block followers if they look like they are trying to 'sell you followers'. They advertise a promise of lots of follows for a few dollars. You will find though, that the followers are just empty accounts and will not add any value to your listings. Some followers only want to use your account to spread their posts of erotica or porn. It is a good tactic to drop in on your account at different times of the day to see what is being shown. I block people if I don't like their content.

Keeping up these actions will steadily build your following. It takes a while, but it is better to do this, than to cheat and pay for lists that are empty users.

How to Navigate the Social Media Maze

There are thousands of accounts on FB, Twitter, and Instagram, etc., that are not actually a *'real person's'* account. They are fake accounts set up by unscrupulous con artists who target desperate people. They sell the possibility of getting hundreds of followers, likes, or hashtag promotions with a promise to increase the popularity of a company or post.

Helpful links

How to spot a fake Twitter account
Fake Twitter accounts
Wikipedia Click Farms

There is a program called Twitteraudit that you can use to Audit your account and check how many fake followers you have. I have about 7.5k followers and when I checked I only had 46 fake fans. You can use it free one time to see how many fake followers you have. However, it does cost money to find out which of your followers are fake, but at 46, I thought I would just leave it at that.

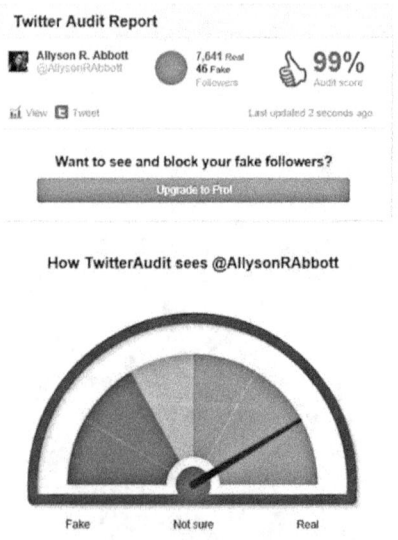

Hashtags #: A few years ago I had no idea what a hashtag was used for. I had very often seen words with hashtags and noticed people talking about them but could never understand the magic. As mentioned previously, Twitter has a list of trends that will allow you to see what is being chatted about or followed. These hashtagged words or terms can be followed by thousands, so it is sometimes a good idea to comment or join in the general conversation, and it may even link to a book or topic you are writing about or your hometown. Using these hashtags could get more visibility for you and your profile. Other social platforms use hashtags as well, but not all.

The use of trend hashtags is good, but there are better hashtags to use. Organizations or groups of people who have a common theme usually create a hashtag to follow. This allows the members or friends who are interested in the subject or topic to search for that hashtag and see what everyone else is tweeting. They can then either respond or retweet.

For example, I have been in some promotion groups for anthologies or general author support and we have a hashtag, if we include it in the 140 characters of the tweet, then other members can easily find the tweets and then retweet to their followers.

One good tip is to find hashtags that link to authors, author support or the genre of your book.

For example #Romance: may find writers and readers of romance. #mustread: will find readers, #amwriting: will link with other writers.

Some support groups like Indie Author Retweet Group has a hashtag of #IARG or #IARTG and, if used in your tweets, other followers of that group could retweet your tweets. There is also Social Networks Retweet Group #SNRG and #Retweetgroup that will help retweet, but you always have to help others by retweeting as well. There is force in numbers and it does work. My sales for my books increase when I use the right hashtags.

How to Navigate the Social Media Maze

Here is a list of hashtags that you could use, but they do take up those valuable characters, so use sparingly.

#Kindle or if your book is in the KDP Select program #KU

#ebooks, #free #giveaway #author #indie #retweet #RT

#ASMSG: Author Social Media Retweet Group

#Bookboost

#Bookpromo

#IAN1: Independent Author Network 1

#EARTG: Erotic Authors Retweet Group

There are lots of different groups for different genres, prices and book retailers. I would advise that after following a few authors within the same genre as you write, to check out their profiles and find the hashtags they use. You can then check to see what group the hashtags are for and follow that.

HashAtlt.com is a hashtag search engine that lets you search for the most popular hashtags on Facebook, Instagram, Pinterest or Twitter. Best of all, it is FREE.

Tweets: Banners, Videos, and gifs: Having an image with your tweet will attract more readers and attention. I spend ages creating banners to promote my tweets. Check the best size to use through the link I provided earlier. You do not use any characters by adding a banner and you can add writing to the banner which will help to explain your tweet. An attractive picture always gains interest. You can also use videos and GIFs. GIFs are a relatively new form of media and are a collection of a few images knitted together to make a short flick through album. You can create with images or words.

Here is an example

Helpful link

Gif Maker

How to Navigate the Social Media Maze

The website above is a good, easy to use site to create an easy GIF. It would be best if you can make a few plain colored plates with a few words on them and then add a few images so there are messages between images. They work well on a lot of SM platforms. Go to the web link and use the 'pictures to GIF' and follow the instructions.

Using the follows, lists, and hashtags, you should be able to build a following and establish a presence on Twitter. Creating colorful and meaningful tweets will help you get retweets and likes. Make sure you retweet others and chat when possible.

Remember to keep checking your notifications to see who retweets and follows you, and reciprocate when possible.

Helpful links

How to Amplify Tweets with hashtags
Twitter Slang and Key Terms

Google Plus (G+)

Having the might of Google behind one of your social media platforms is a good idea. With their search engines and algorithms, their ability to track and interact is phenomenal. If possible, I also suggest you use other Google tools as well, like Google analytics for your website, and Adsense and Adwords. The more you get involved with Google, the more you will be seen.

There is the argument that Google (and to a certain extent MSN) are extremely invasive and start to take over your digital life. So, at the end of the day, you need to decide how much you want them to get involved.

How to Navigate the Social Media Maze

One of the main reasons you have a G+ account is so you can share posts with your fans and gain a larger network. To do this you need to use your G+ URL and the available icons, like these;

Helpful link

Flat icons.com

You can use a hyperlink with the image to direct people to your SM accounts from your other platforms and in your SM (stalker) links.

You can customize your G+ URL (mine is http://google.com/+AllysonRAbbott) once you have had a Google Plus account for thirty days or more and have followed their requirements. Rather than me explaining what you have to do, it is better if you follow this link (which will be up to date) and then follow the steps.

Get a Custom URL for your Google+ Profile

I have a Google account and use Blogger, Drive, Maps, Docs, Translate, YouTube, and of course, Google search. I do not have a Gmail account, although I probably will eventually. My husband does not like the power of Google and prefers to use Bing for searches. Google searches are good enough for me and I always find what I need. I haven't even updated to Google Chrome yet, which does mean I am a bit behind in some technology available. If I like what I have, I don't like to change just because the new version comes along.

So, how does G+ help you as an author?

It's another platform where you can interact with authors and book lovers and meet up with like-minded people. Setting up a profile is easy and you determine what personal information you share. G+ is like FB and Twitter, where you can post images and information to share with others, you follow people and get followers. Whereas FB has groups, G+ has 'Communities'.

How to Navigate the Social Media Maze

On your 'Home' page you will see a stream of information from the people you follow. Unlike FB or Twitter, you can see more than one post at a time (similar to Pinterest) in three columns and each post can have text, images, videos, gifs, etc. On the homepage, you can add your own posts and images to share with others, or share and comment on their posts. When posting, you can choose if you want to make the post public, to everyone who follows you, or to a particular 'circle'.

Circles and People: You can also create 'Circles' to separate your diffcrent contacts. When you open an account it will come with three pre-named circles, 'Friends, Family, and Acquaintances', you can rename them and create different ones, maybe for clubs, or work or beta readers or fans, etc. You can add people to more than one circle, so they can be your work colleague and a friend, and you can interact with each circle differently. Again like Facebook and Twitter, you can follow people who do not follow you back.

When you follow someone you have to add them to a circle, so it is a good idea to have the circles already created and possibly have a 'miscellaneous' or 'other' circle for those you want to follow, but not sure which circle they fit into until you have checked out their profile.

For example, on the People tab (to the left on your homepage) you will find three lists: who you Follow, your Followers and Find People.

If you view your 'followers list', under each of their pictures you will see if you already follow them or not and which circle you have slotted them into.

If you don't follow them, there will be a button that says 'follow'. As it's polite to follow back, this is a good place to find if you have missed anyone. If you select to follow someone but then are not sure who they are or what they do, it's hard to know which circle to add them to; as this process is done at the same time as you follow. Therefore, I suggest you either check into each profile first, but this takes time, or have a general circle for 'new friends', or 'new connections', and pop them in there, until you see what they post, or find out which of your circles will suit them better.

On occasion you can get some weirdo following you, so you do need to be a bit choosy in what you allow them to have access to. A general circle, with no personal information shared, is a good place to start for unknowns.

If you click on the 'Find People' tab, it will show you a list of people who are following some of your contacts. These are 'people in common'. Don't be fooled into thinking all these suggestions are legit. If you checked on some, they may not have posted for years, or they have made inappropriate posts. I know it takes time, but I would check first before you follow, or make a list of friends from FB, or other groups or social media you are involved in, or even authors of books that you read.

Google+ Communities: As mentioned earlier G+ Communities work like Groups on FB, where users with things in common come together and share, discuss or post items of interest.

These communities are about blogging, but there are plenty more about authors, books and possibly genre related. As you can see by the membership numbers, they are definitely worth posting about your books once in a while. If you don't like FB, then this could be an alternative without all the chats, likes and advertisements that interrupt your news and post feeds, although you do need to communicate and not just post about your books if you want to build a following.

My thoughts on G+

Whereas it is neat and tidy and not as distracting as FB, I find it a little limiting on what you can do and it isn't very 'user-friendly' when trying to go back and forth between tabs. It is good to have a profile and to make sure the G+ icon is everywhere you can place it as this shows you have a healthy social media platform. There are thousands of users with whom you can connect and, if you build a following, it is as good as having a newsletter. You could always check for responses by putting a giveaway on there (and not anywhere else). If it proves your posts are being read, then good. If not, then only post occasionally, or work harder at gaining some trust and followers, if you want to use it as a main platform. As mentioned previously, having a presence on a Google platform can only help.

Helpful link

Welcome to the Google+ Help Center

Pinterest

A word of warning, you can lose hours on Pinterest.

It took me a couple of years to even bother opening an account, as I couldn't see what all the fuss was about. Who wants to spend time just looking at pictures? This is what I thought it all boiled down to. How wrong I was. This is now my go-to place when looking for recipes, knitting patterns, anything to do with crafts, weddings, and, of course, books and writing. My problem is time, since I spend too much time looking at stuff and not enough time developing my profile, boards, and followers. I think Pinterest has magic powers. You can get lost in the magical world.

It is easy to create an account and I suggest creating a business/professional account as an author, making sure you use the tag 'author' in your name. A business account allows you to link to other web or sales pages, where you can try and engage more with followers.

You can create boards (naming them what you want) and pin relevant images to them. Think of it as having lots of cork boards around your house and each cork board is dedicated to a theme. You can also add an image to more than one board. There is no limit to how many images you add. Other users can pin your images to their boards as well. The good thing is, you can also peek at everyone's boards and pin any of their pictures to your boards. Even though they are pictures/images, most of them are linked to websites where you can obtain information about the image. I like cooking and my husband is a vegan, so I am always looking for new recipes and Pinterest is a wealth of information. It is easy to link pins to a blog or website.

You can add the Pinterest Browser Button to your favorite browser. This allows you to pin an image to a Pinterest board directly, from wherever you find it. This button is free and makes keeping your Pinterest account active and up-to-date as simple as a click of your mouse.

How does this help Authors?

After setting up an account (which has your website or FB page as your URL), use the search bar to find boards or posts that interest you or link to your genre, books or local town. Follow a few to help you become visible. If you like a pin then save it by clicking on the save it sign and then add it to one of your boards. You can create as many boards as you want and name them appropriately. Try to think of a name that will resonate with other readers or book lovers so they may find your boards and then follow them or you.

The key to Pinterest is to get as many followers as possible to your boards, or one board, so when you post a new pin they will get a notification.

If you can attract users to your profile they will probably check out all your other boards. Upload images of your book covers or banners advertising your books, to your appropriately named boards, making sure you add the URL to your page or a sales link for your book. You can send interested readers to your website or blog, so they can get to know you, or directly to Amazon.

I don't think you can just use Pinterest as a means of promoting, but as another string to the social media bow, it is worth keeping in touch and adding a few images during the week. You can join boards (which are like groups) and there is also a website called BoardBooster, which will help pin and publicize your boards for you.

Helpful link

Boardbooster

I have to admit to not knowing an awful lot about this site, apart from the fact it has some great tools (not all free) and it helps to keep me in the loop with other boards. I actually pay someone from Fiverr.com to attend to my Pinterest Account every few months to make sure I am on track. She was the one who introduced me to BoardBooster and whatever she did works wonders. I am scared to log in too often on Pinterest as I disappear into the unknown realms of craft making and recipes. I pin my covers and banners with my eyes shut!

It is good to have a presence on Pinterest as it helps build your brand, and if you write in a genre aimed at women readers, there is a good chance they are on Pinterest too.

You can pay for promotions to gain visibility.

My thoughts on Pinterest

I like it as a platform for gathering information for my personal use. Which, in theory, should mean I can give information to others to attract them to my book, but the giving is harder than the taking.

If you got into the swing and created a folder where you regularly slotted all the images/banners or book covers you are using that week for other promotions, and then went once a week to Pinterest and uploaded them onto the relevant boards, it may work. In fact, I might even follow my own advice and try that out. I get on Pinterest and spend too much time dipping and diving into my files and folders looking for new stuff to pin, therefore I tend to not do it.

Pinterest does have a huge following.

How to Navigate the Social Media Maze

I (Donna) invite you to follow me on Pinterest.

https://www.pinterest.com/specialangel87/

I have a board, Writing, devoted to writing tips and grammar. There is a lot of useful information right at your fingertips. Head on over and check it out.

Helpful links

How to Use Pinterest 2017

Pinterest Marketing

How to Use Pinterest **video**

Understand What Pinterest is all About

How to Use Pinterest

LinkedIn

It seems only natural to have a LinkedIn account. Everyone else seems to have one, so it must be good! Like most social media platforms, LinkedIn has its purpose, and some of those would be job hunting, marketing, and building connections. I would say that LinkedIn works extremely well for businesses and does need dedication to plan a good marketing strategy. However, as an author, you could also use the tools and the thousands of users to promote yourself and your books.

If you were looking for editors, graphic designers, or publishers this would also be a good place to start. One of the main benefits for authors is that no matter the reason other people sign up for LinkedIn, the majority of them will be readers. Readers love books, so you can promote or discuss your books, offer giveaways and you will find someone interested in your goods, even if they do not interact with you. This does make it hard to judge if LinkedIn is worth spending time on.

How to Navigate the Social Media Maze

Setting up a profile on LinkedIn is a little more complicated than other platforms because it asks for more history and information; which is to be expected for career purposes. You can upload your resume and use the platform to hunt for jobs, and generally any advancement within the realm of work.

This platform is mainly for professional job hunters and advertising vacancies, so I tend to only check in once in a while. If you are a marketer and have time to plan a good strategy, LinkedIn would be a very good place to start. Although classed as an SM platform, it mainly focuses on professionalism and uses commonality to connect people, rather than just for fun or for a chat.

On this platform, you build a 'network' by 'connecting' with people. Your homepage is very similar to other platforms with your stream of news in the middle from the people you have connected with. Along the top, there are tabs for your 'network, jobs, messaging, notifications, and me'; along the right is also an extension to the LinkedIn tools for job hunting and posting solutions.

As with other platforms, the more people you connect with the more people will see your posts. So again, the idea is to build up relationships with others, especially book lovers, authors or other elements within the publishing industry. What is not a good idea on LinkedIn, is to post too many repetitive adverts for your book. Use this media a little more subtly. Post about needing an editor, beta readers, and reviewers or asking for help with some aspect of writing/promoting your books. You may not get many replies, but your face (brand) and book will be seen and hopefully remembered. Not all marketing is about direct sales, it can be about subliminal messages.

My advice would be to have a free LinkedIn account (you can go professional for a monthly fee) and to make connections, join a few groups, chat with some people, respond to their career changes etc., but only pop in once or maybe twice a week to post about an event or a plea for help.

My thoughts on LinkedIn

With such a huge following it would be unwise to ignore it, but as a platform for promoting your books, it is hard to say if it benefits you or not as you are generally sending them to a sales platform. You could do a 'special LinkedIn' offer and see what the response is to judge if you are being seen or making connections. As a place for finding professional help with the elements of writing and publishing, you can't go wrong, and it certainly will not hinder your social media profile by having a LinkedIn account. Keep in mind, it really does not need a lot of input to keep it going once you have your account set up.

Helpful links

Book Promotion Strategies for Authors
Tips on how get LinkedIn to work for Authors
4 reasons why Authors should use LinkedIn

I have recently learned of another SM site, [MeWe - Next-Gen Social Network](#).

Several authors that I follow are giving it a try and encouraging their friends and fans to do the same. While it isn't a well-known SM site, it might be a good idea to give it a try, or at least be aware it is available.

From MeWe's website:

- MeWe challenges the status quo by making privacy the foundation of online social experiences.
- MeWe keeps your information free from tracking, spying, and scraping.
- MeWe is where you can be authentic and uncensored, the way you are in your real life.

They state you get to determine who sees your posts, not some algorithm or arbitrary nonsense. No one can report your posts just because they don't like them. Your trust and safety are at the heart of MeWe.

Section 5:
Book Cataloging
& Social Networking Sites

If you don't like the idea of using Facebook and Twitter to help promote your books or to network with other authors, then Goodreads and LibraryThing could be a good alternative. You still need to have some other platform to expose your books and yourself to the outside world, like a blog or website. You would be able to expose your books to book lovers and gain feedback, without having to interact and post on a regular basis. Keeping communication to a minimum with your readers and fans, and if they spread the word, your following could soon start to grow.

You could still have accounts on other SM platforms and let them tick over by posting every now and again or even by having a personal assistant to post for you.

I know not everyone likes using FB, as they find it invasive and extremely time-consuming.

Using book sharing platforms is a good way for new writers to build confidence and a following. Apart from Goodreads and LibraryThing, which have a huge following from all demographics, you also need to consider Wattpad. There are others, like Reddit.com, but this is also very distracting as it has so many links and loops which encourage videos and instant reaction. **Shelfari** was another good author/book webpage/app, but was taken over by Amazon and after a while closed down.

Before I started writing, I had never come across Goodreads or LibraryThing. I had heard of **Wattpad;** which originated in 2006, mainly as an app for smartphones, and 85% of its traffic and usage comes from mobile devices (see HERE). This is probably why Wattpad attracts a younger audience of writers and readers. They were the first generation to soak up all the new technology as it happened.

How to Navigate the Social Media Maze

Goodreads was founded in 2006 with a stated mission "to help people find and share books they love' (see HERE). Their main development was focused on its website and aimed at readers, rather than budding writers, like Wattpad.

LibraryThing was the first of these social cataloging websites to get up and running (2005). They imported thousands of book details from registered book lists, although you can add your own if it's not on a list yet.

What is good to remember is that all this happened before the indie movement swept ashore. Kindle Direct Publishing (Amazon's ebook publishing arm) did not launch until 2007, so these 'book and writing' sharing websites have had to play catch up and react fairly quickly to the millions of new and emerging authors and books. Amazon purchased a 40% share of LibraryThing in May 2006, obviously knowing they were on to a good thing.

So, let's find out a few basics about each of these platforms and how they can help you as an author. If you like the idea of setting up accounts and using these as your main arrowhead, then I would suggest looking for a book that can help with more details than we have space to write here. We are supplying the basics for you to decide if further investigation is needed.

Wattpad

If I could start my writing career again, or if I was younger and not in such a hurry, I would definitely have used Wattpad (it now has over 45 million users). It's easy to join, easy to use and it could help you build a following even before you publish a book.

You can publish snippets from a book, and ask for feedback, or publish chapters at a time to get readers hooked and encourage discussions and sharing. For new and aspiring authors, it is a great place to learn and develop your craft.

Next year I am planning to write a series of books, before publishing any of them, and I am considering Wattpad as the teaser playground.

Wattpad has communities and contests and you can follow writers, genres or themes; whatever you like. The aim for the writer is to get as many likes as possible; to make the top of the charts, so the more you are seen, the more likes you will get, the more people will follow you.

It is known that some writers who started on Wattpad, have ended up with book deals and even television series. Wattpad is more than just reading and posting your pages, it can also support you in other ventures; check their 'about page'.

As the average time users spend on the app or website is thirty minutes, it is best to keep any writing contributions short in order to keep a reader's full attention. As most readers get through 25 -30 pages (in a native language) in half an hour, an upload of one or two chapters at a time is ideal, but don't forget they have to find you first, unless they already follow you.

My suggestion is to sign up and take a look around and read some of the work that is on there. Take notice of how many follows some of the favorite writers have and check out their work. It is important to make sure all the work you load onto Wattpad is edited and formatted to offer the best reading experience. Bad reviews can be scathing and it may take a while to gain back any readers

How to Navigate the Social Media Maze

Although you will not gain any direct sales from Wattpad, it is an ideal launching pad for a career and is a great place to gain followers and fans. This is especially true if you are a new young writer, who can relate to the new technology. There is no harm in having a go at any age, but you would probably need to write to attract the Teenage, Young Adult or New Adult audience. Wattpad prides themselves on having 'the millennials' attention.'

> *"Our users are youthful, always connected, and they engage with our content for an average of 30 minutes per session. Millennials and Gen Z make up 90% of our total monthly audience of 45 million people."*

They even have a 'connection' service, where they connect you with some of their talented writers who will collaborate with you to write your story. They can also link your story to advertisers to bring more publicity. Not to be sneezed at. As mentioned, it could be a way to promote you and your books if your face and stories fit their platform. I for one encourage all new writers to seriously think about it, even if it's as a trial.

How to Navigate the Social Media Maze

Goodreads and LibraryThing

Both of these deserve a mention, although, I'm not sure if you would class them as SM or book lovers paradise. On both GR and LT you can sign up either as a reader or an author, but I believe you need to be a reader before you can sign up as an author.

Each site has thousands of readers and book lovers. The idea, as a reader, is that you read and review books and share your reviews. You can support other readers and authors. Your listed books can be ebooks or paperbacks. Since GR is owned by AZ, they will very helpfully connect your AZ account with GR for easier listing, if you want to do that. Your books from your AZ account can be imported to your GR shelves. Then to make it even easier for LT, you can import all your books from GR over to LT fairly easily. It took me one minute, and I had 344 books on my reading shelves. It also imports the reviews and ratings.

Allyson R. Abbott & Donna Wolz

On the flip side (from Donna)

There is a downside to connecting GR and LT to FB and AZ. This lets AZ peek into your FB profile. If AZ determines you have a 'relationship' with an author based on your FB interactions, they will remove reviews you have written for that author. No, it doesn't make any sense. You follow an author and interact with them because you are a fan. You are not close personal friends with every author you chat with on FB. I can assure you, AZ won't listen to any explanation. They cannot be reasoned with. The irony is, they don't remove your GR reviews. I guess relationships don't matter to AZ all the time.

I have personally had my reviews removed from numerous authors' books because I supported and promoted them. I do consider a few authors friends, but reviews I wrote before I ever talked to them have been removed. There is no rhyme or reason to AZ's policy. It is totally arbitrary.

How to Navigate the Social Media Maze

There are Giveaways to sign up for as a reader or you can create one to get your book noticed (paperback and ebooks).

In LibraryThing you can give away up to 100 ebooks in one event. I have to admit that although I have a presence on both, Goodreads never used to allow ebooks as giveaways, only paperbacks. I have given away my fair share of both. Last year (I believe) GR also started a beta ebook giveaway, which I attempted to sign up for, but gave up when I discovered you had to pay $100 to do so. I couldn't see the point in paying to give away books when I could do a few free days on KDP Select for nothing. After checking recently there does not appear to be any ebook giveaways on GR, hmmm I wonder why! Either the beta test did not work, or authors are too wise.

The whole point of book giveaways is to hopefully gain followers and reviews for your book while getting your name seen. For me, neither of these platforms have garnered many reviews from book giveaways.

I do use GR more than LT, as I find it a little more user-friendly. However, I do find both platforms clumsy to use as an author, consequently, I'm sure I don't spend enough time to gain any benefit from it. I do try and post reviews for books that I read and connect to people through other social media platforms, but I am still trying to find the best way to harness my followers to help increase sales.

There are groups you can join and it's easy to create a group. I know that some authors create groups for their books and try to interact more with readers. I have joined groups that will benefit me and I have also created a group to support my preferred writing genre.

What you need to keep in mind is that both these websites were initially set up for readers to share their love of books, to write and publish reviews and to find out about new books. That being said, they are good platforms for authors, (especially as they are both linked to Amazon) but you are encouraged not to contact readers to request reviews, but you can tell everyone about your new books and encourage honest reviews. Everything has to be kept subtle, or you could be removed.

Goodreads in brief

Goodreads is a good place to set up an author account. They have 55 million members, 1.5 billion books listed on their site, and over 50 million reviews. GR is a great way to promote your books. Plus, it is FREE to set up your author profile and list your book(s).

Goodreads allows books to be reviewed before they are published and the review can easily be posted/shared to FB and Twitter. This allows people to see how others are reacting to your book before it is released. If it is on pre-order, this can lead to more sales so that on release day, AZ takes notice, especially if the reviewers post the review to AZ, after publication. Getting AZ to take notice of your book is important because, once they do, there are different ways they will promote your book for FREE.

If you created and published your paperback copy, prior to your ebook, you could do giveaways, and request reviews from your followers or fan club early.

Have readers follow you on GR and add your book to their To Be Read (TBR) shelf. If readers follow you,

How to Navigate the Social Media Maze

GR will notify them of your new releases, sales, and any GR promotions you may undertake. You could also create an 'event' for your release day. Your followers are automatically notified of any activities: another easy, FREE way to get information about your books out to readers.

When someone reviews your book on GR, make sure you acknowledge the post. All it takes is to hit the 'Like' button. This is a simple way to let people know you appreciate them for reading and reviewing your book(s).

How to create your author page

It's simple to create your author page. Simply create a Goodreads account. Then search for your book by ISBN, ASIN, or title. Once you find your book, click on your name on the book description and you will be taken to your author profile. Update as needed and you are ready to go.

Goodreads Author Program

Adding books to Goodreads

If your book isn't in Goodreads' database, you can manually add your book.

Only a GR Librarian can manually add books if your account is less than a week old. In that case, contact the Goodreads Librarians group.

If your account is not new, you can add your book manually

Goodreads offers several ways to promote your book.

Giveaways are a great way to get readers' attention. Everyone loves getting something for FREE. Follow this link to learn how to set up a giveaway.

To get the most from your Goodreads Giveaway, they have some helpful tips at:

Giveaway best Practices

How to Navigate the Social Media Maze

One of the benefits of the giveaways is that most entrants tick a box (or they probably don't bother unticking it) that automatically puts the book they are requesting in the giveaway onto their 'want to read' shelf. So your book could get a lot more visibility. You can get hundreds of people signing up, but what is a real shame is that you are not allowed to contact those who did not win. I really wanted to let them know about a 'free' day I was having a few months later. However, as a negative point to these paperback giveaways, when I'd check the profiles for the readers who had placed my book on their 'want to read' shelf, I couldn't help but notice quite a few of them had thousands of books on the same shelf and hardly any friends, reviews or ratings to their name. It made me recognize the fact that a lot of GR members signing up for free paperback giveaways are only in it for the book and have no intention of reading and reviewing. There are of course many honest book lovers and I just hoped they were the ones who won my books.

Ask the Author: Encourage your followers to post questions and/or comments in the Ask the Author section. Be sure to respond within a reasonable amount of time. This is another way to interact with your readers on a more personal level. It gives them insight into your books and lets them learn a little about you.

Announcements: To announce an upcoming release, sale, or giveaway, write a blog post or post a status update. This will appear in the news feed of your followers. You can even connect your blog to your GR account.

Events: You can set up an event on GR. This is another way to get people to sign up for things like Blog Tours or Blog Hops.

Helpful link

Creating an Event

Advertising: You can advertise on Goodreads. It does cost money, but you can target a specific audience so your advertising will be more effective.

How to Navigate the Social Media Maze

Helpful link

Goodreads Advertisers

Help for advertisers

Goodreads cautions authors to never send readers private messages. They also warn against over-promoting your book(s) by joining too many groups and constantly posting information about your book(s). If you over-promote your books, it comes across as spam and no one wants to see spam.

Do try to remember that GR is mainly for readers, and hopefully, you are a reader, so you need to support other authors and write reviews for their work and also share on SM. It may attract others to your profile and you could gain more visibility.

There are a few books on how authors can get the best out of GR. I am not going to endorse any particular one, but I do recommend buying one if you want to try and use Goodreads as one of your main connecting platforms.

Helpful links

How to Promote Your Books on Goodreads

8 Ways Authors can use Goodreads

10 Sites like Goodreads for Authors and Readers

LibraryThing in brief

This is another platform primarily for readers, and then it seems as an afterthought for authors. It has lots of features and statistics, a good community for asking questions and receiving answers, groups, recommendations, giveaways and an Early-bird Review program. Don't get too excited about this last feature as it not available to indie authors. You can, however, use the giveaway feature and put up one hundred books to give away. Once the giveaway has ended you get a nice email from the admin telling you it has finished. Then you need to go and find the list of winners in the 'early-bird and giveaway' section, which did take me a long while to find. It is this problem with LT that makes me hesitate to fully recommend it as a potential platform for networking, as the 'user friendliness' of it isn't the best. Don't get me wrong, it has huge potential and again if you don't like the idea of FB, Twitter, and other SM platforms, but love to be surrounded by readers and authors, then this could be just for you. I would suggest though that you take a week out of your life to fully understand the tools, features and the ethics of this social cataloging platform.

My usual port of call, if I have problems understanding a website is to go and find a book on it. I can't find a book on LT to help me. I may even spend a week out of my life learning all about it and write one myself.

As a reader you can upload your book lists and reviews and ratings, search for recommendations, authors, titles, etc. and join groups, apply for giveaways and early review opportunities and generally interact with other members and have fun. There are statistics to browse and lots of information to learn.

So what can it do for you as an author?

You need to have an account first before you can open an author profile.

You can upload or claim your books, see how many reviews you have, how many members have your book listed under their profiles, join groups, do giveaways and everything you expect from a website of this magnitude.

How to Navigate the Social Media Maze

Giveaways: Posting a giveaway for a paperback, ebooks or audiobooks is very simple.

Groups: There are numerous groups you can search through and join, but do not expect to be able to promote your book.

Talk: There are a multitude of topics and chats that you can join in with, as well as lots of help you can get. The more you join in, the more people will see your name and hopefully follow you and check out your books.

Location: You can add your geographical location to help you link with local events, libraries, and bookstores, etc. (great for setting up a book signing event).

And then they have the Zeitgeist Overview, which they boldly state is 'More information than you require.'

This following section is just the start of it and you will see why they make that statement.

Allyson R. Abbott & Donna Wolz

Vital Statistics

Members 2,208,982

Books catalogued 117,609,050

Tags added 137,385,723

Unique works held 11,099,687

Unique works total 19,719,477

Reviews 3,109,709

Works reviewed 1,083,437

Ratings 17,682,860

Member-contributed covers 5,302,297

Author pictures 106,906

Venue pictures 15,341

Groups 11,224

Talk topics 194,366

Talk messages 6,137,218

Talk touchstones 4,591,723

Free books given out

Early Reviewer books given out 299,831

Member Giveaway books given out 906,336

Total free books given out 1,206,167

How to Navigate the Social Media Maze

It continues on with the largest libraries, top books, top reviews, top rated, lowest rated; you name it, it's rated. As mentioned earlier, LT does seem to like statistics. I am a great statistics lover and enjoy browsing through some of the information.

I just cannot warm up to the site. It seems to me to be overly complicated and I just don't have enough time to do all the tools and facilities justice, but they are there to be used. On each page there is a help tab, tucked away on the top right, and there are groups, chats, and pages where you can get help. It is that old adage: you don't need any help if you don't know what it is you can't do.

So, I suggest you roll up your sleeves, get a glass of wine or coffee and spend a few hours just checking through the website to see if you feel confident enough to ask questions and to dive in.

Helpful links

How Authors can use LibraryThing

Other Author and Book Listing platforms to consider

The Independent Author Network: (IAN) is a community of authors who are self-published or published by a small indie press.
Costs: One-time fee involved.

Scribed: Document Sharing Site - self-publishing platform -can publish to it through Smashwords or Bookbaby. You can link to your website—when 30% of your book is read it's a sale -authors can get 60% or 70% of a sale.
Costs: None for authors to sign up - subscription cost for readers

Redditt: A collection of user communities, get more viewership of your book, get feedback from readers.
Costs: None

Lean Pub: Document Sharing - publish serial fiction or full books to find readers– they can be free or cost money for readers.
Costs: None

How to Navigate the Social Media Maze

Deviantart: For publishing poetry or short stories only- not for longer works.

Costs: none

Quotev: Document sharing site - post **fanfics** and original stories - get more viewership of your book, get feedback from readers - good for fantasy.

Costs: none

FanFiction.Net: Document sharing site - Writers upload their fan fiction stories —get more viewership of your book, and get reviews from readers.

Costs: none

Penana: Document sharing in serial and collaborative formats —for young and aspiring writers —get feedback.

Costs: none

BookLikes: Promote your books to a community of over 40K readers, reviewers, and book bloggers.

Costs: none

Third Scribe: Provides book pages, author listings, reviews, author websites, and forums. Post links, pictures, videos, and get member reviews.

Cost for authors - free to premium package at $54.99

Section 6:
Social Media Management Systems
& Other Tools

As an indie author, you are soon made aware of the huge task of promoting your books. The more books you write the more promoting you need to do, and the more time it takes. The introduction of social media management systems was a boon, but now there are so many on the market, which all do basically the same thing with different approaches. This means it takes time to choose or learn how to use them.

A few years ago there were a couple to choose from, but now the selection has expanded somewhat, with quite a few offering tools for analytics as an enticement. They have gone from tweet automation services to wider social media platforms with analytics, **SEO** advice, and **metadata linking**.

Whereas they are useful, I think the main thing for authors is to actually get the word out about the books first and then perhaps check to see who is reading the messages and what time of day is more fruitful. Also, most tweet automation systems will include posting to other social media platforms as well.

The whole idea for me of SM management systems is to save time. I could spend ages posting on FB and Twitter, so having a platform that allows bulk uploads or to schedule a week in advance for multi posts, is extremely helpful. Everyone will have their reasons for choosing a particular one, but with so many to explain, I will only go into detail for the most popular and list the rest with links for you to do your own investigation. Making a decision will really depend on whether you are looking to get the best out of your SM posts, to find a system to manage all posts with reports, or to save time.

Actually, the first one I am going to list is not in the well-known section. Twittimer is the one I use because I found it straightforward and uncomplicated. I had an account on Buffer and Hootsuite but struggled to understand what I was doing and why I couldn't schedule the same post for another time. They may have changed their system since then or maybe it was just not simple enough for me to cope with, after all, I am an author, not an IT guru. I remember emailing Buffer on the same issue for two to three weeks, trying to fathom out my problem, and although they replied, it just didn't make sense to me. Hootsuite, just looked complicated, when all I wanted to do was schedule posts.

To give you a taste of what is to come in this section, I thought it would be more constructive if I put the helpful links first to allow you to have a peek at the possible management systems.

Helpful links

10 Best Social Media Management Applications
Social Media Examiner: 5 tools to save time
17 Best Social Media Management Tools
The Best Social Media Analytical Tools
Ranking of Best Social Media Management Software
Dashburst Blog: The best SM management tools

The above web links will give you a good oversight of the available tools. You need to read a few to get a good, unbiased idea. Some focus on automation and management and others are more aimed for businesses with lots of analytical tools. As an independent author and publisher, you are, in theory, a small business, but while all the extras offer great insight for your publicity drives, they take a lot of time to analyze.

So, what should I use? Whatever you like!

Twittimer

I was reading a blog post by an author who said she used Twittimer. Having never heard of it, I took a look. I really liked the simplicity of their website, and after a quick scan of the menu, including their services and prices, I joined up for the 'Pro' option, although you can try it out at the 'Free Basic' level first.

You can sign up with either your Twitter or FB accounts, or your LinkedIn profile, and then you can add more profiles or pages within these accounts if you have them. For example, I have a few FB pages and three Twitter accounts, but I can schedule posts to each of those, or the same post to all, take your pick. I also post to my LinkedIn account.

Recently, Twittimer, added an analytical tool to each post so you can see how many times it was shared and the reach of that post, without having to do any research.

For each post, you can upload an image and insert your text, then attach it to the profile where you want it to post. If you are over the text limit for that platform, it will let you know. You can schedule posts to fit your needs.

Once it has been posted, it will be seen in the archived section (which all posts are available for 60 days) and from there you can reschedule your posts to any time in the future. I try to keep a week in front, but sometimes it's only days. If I know I am going to be away from home, then I will do two weeks in advance and not worry about it.

I use a spreadsheet to keep all my posts listed (a tab for each book or topic) and a number in the image column, so I know which image to attach to each post. This way

I know the same post will not be posted within 24 hrs of each other (which is not allowed, or it is called spam by Twitter), and the images are fresh each day.

You do need to spend a bit of time setting up all the tweets and images in the right folders on your PC for easy access, but once done, rescheduling it is much easier. Previously I spent about 10/15 minutes a day doing all the reschedules. Now I pay someone each month to reschedule my posts for me. This way it saves me time, I can spend more time on creating new banners and actually spend more time on my writing and forget about tweets.

There are some tools that I don't use. One is the bulk uploading of your posts via a **CSV file**, and the other one allows you to set up fixed times of the week for posts to go out, so it saves time each week. I like to mix the times up, so as not to bore the same readers at the same time each week, but it is up to each individual.

Helpful links

Twittimer Pricing
A Bloggers Review of Twittimer

How to Navigate the Social Media Maze

Buffer

Although Buffer was not available until a year or so after Hootsuite, it is a very popular and visible media management system. Its name probably helps, as it sounds friendlier than Hootsuite.

It has different levels available. Choose whether you want the free basic, the awesome, or the business. There are more tools available with each successive level. The free version limits you to 10 posts per week, so most authors would probably go for the Awesome package, which costs $102 a year or $10 a month. Instead of the 10 free posts a week, you can then schedule 100. Awesome also includes Twitter, FB, Instagram, Pinterest, LinkedIn, and G+ as options to post to with 10 social profiles allowed. The free option only allows 5.

I am trying to remember why I didn't like Buffer and I think it's because I wanted to share the same post to different media platforms, but they only post to one at a time. This may have changed and I would suggest trying the free version.

Allyson R. Abbott & Donna Wolz

Helpful links

Buffer Prices and Plans

How to Navigate the Social Media Maze

Hootsuite

Hootsuite was started in 2008, originally under the name of Brightkit, but was changed to Hootsuite within a year. The Hootsuite platform has a lot of high profile users and followers and offers a lot of tools and interaction for businesses. Their dashboard can be used as a hub for all social media profiles, instead of having to check into each one separately. I think it was this activity that decided for me that it was too invasive and disruptive to my lifestyle. I did not necessarily want to see all the action on my social media platforms all the time---I just wanted to post to them. You can add more streams if needed.

Their prices are a bit steep, but you do get a lot for your money if you want all the information and tools on hand.

You can sign up for a 30-day free trial, which I recommend. Their basic package is $16 a month for 10 social profiles.

Helpful links

Hootsuite Prices

Clear Voice: Hootsuite v Buffer

UK Linkology: Hootsuite v Buffer

How to Navigate the Social Media Maze

There are a lot more social media management or automation platforms, and the best way to decide is for you to check out a few. As there are so many comparisons out there already, and a lot of information, it would only add another dimension if I tried to explain all the differences as well.

Here is a helpful link that compares quite a few:

We Rock Your Web

I have listed some of the most popular ones here:

TweetDeck It's owned by Twitter. It's free. For Twitter only. You can schedule your posts. It doesn't offer any stats or reporting options.

TweetDeck is an extremely useful program, which helps to organize your Twitter account or accounts into columns of activities. If you have more than one profile and want to keep up with all the notifications, messages or trending hashtags, this is the place for you. You can tweet directly from here as well as schedule (by creating a column for scheduling). If you want to schedule a lot of posts well in advance, then perhaps it is not the best option, but for planning daily tweets and checking messages daily, it is a great option. It does look a bit busy, as all your streams in your created columns will be moving and changing, but you can cut out the ones that are not important and just keep an eye on what you want.

Helpful links

Is TweetDeck only for Twitter?

TweetDeck v Hootsuite

TweetDeck; How to Schedule tweets

Social Juke Box: Formerly known as Tweetjukebox, it manages posts to Twitter, Facebook, and LinkedIn. Price structure ranges from free to $99 a month.

Socialbakers: It analyzes social media data so you can see the benchmark for your own social media promotions to let you manage your Twitter and Facebook ads in one place.

Socialoomph: It manages your social media on multiple accounts and platforms. It has an auto-follower and a manual unfollow feature. But no live feed feature. It's analytical and auto responding feature is great. They offer a free trial period.

How to Navigate the Social Media Maze

Sproutsocial: It manages your social media like Hootsuite and others. It handles Facebook, LinkedIn, RSS, & Twitter. It's well organized. It has built-in CRM (customer relationship manager) so you can create a list of keywords and monitor them. It has an auto-scheduling queue feature. It's more expensive - $99 per month.

Twuffer: It schedules tweets, but like Buffer, you don't need to enter the time. It sets the time-zone you're in and sends out your tweets from your queue. It can track tweets that didn't get sent out.

Zoho Social: It manages your social media; similar to Hootsuite, but Zoho offers online support, with packages ranging from free to $50 a month. They have many additional features not found on a lot of other platforms, including automated scheduling, keyword tracking, social media metrics and lots more.

AgoraPulse: A good all in one social management tool, with your social media accounts under one dashboard—looks like a mobile phone screen. It puts all messages sent to you in one box and all messages about you in another. It has an advanced social monitoring feature that works like Google Alerts. Pricing information: AgoraPulsePricing. It looks to be more for business than individuals

Everypost: It manages your Twitter and other social media - lets you post on Facebook, Google +, & LinkedIn. It lets you add YouTube videos and mp4 files and for music links; Grooveshar and mp3 files. It's got photo editing features and you can pull photos from within the app, your camera files, Flickr, and Instagram.

Falcon Social: Falcon Social is a social media management site that is mainly for teams to collaborate on Facebook, Twitter, Google+, Instagram, and YouTube profiles. At the top end of marketing and starts at $1000 a month

Gremlin Social: It's a lot like Hootsuite. It lets you monitor several social media platforms at one time. No visible price list and you need to fill in a form to request a demo.

Mavsocial: It's a social media management tool for Twitter, Facebook, Google+, LinkedIn, and Foursquare. It has a free plan to manage Twitter and Facebook posts. It has a social inbox which lets you see all your social engagements. And it has an interactive reporting dashboard with a range of metrics. Find pricing information here. Mavsocial pricing

Allyson R. Abbott & Donna Wolz

Tools for Managing Specific Social Media Platforms

What else is available?

Apart from the options above for managing and tracking your social media posts, you also have other tools/programs that can help monitor and expand followers, friends, or boards and are dedicated to specific social media platforms.

Crowdfire : This is an application that can be linked and used with your Twitter and Instagram accounts. When it originally launched in Feb 2010, it was known as 'JustUnfollow'. However, in Feb 2015 it was re-branded to Crowdfire.

I use the free version for my Twitter account. So, what does it do? It helps you to grow your following through visibility of who follows and who is inactive.

On your dashboard page, you can see the data of how many followers you have and who you are following. So does Twitter, I hear you say, but here it is easy to unfollow, to see who is inactive over the past 1-6 months and to find followers of people you follow, all on one easy to use page. It automatically links to the account that you set it up to and gathers data every time you log on.

I have to mention that recently it has altered its homepage and set up. When I created a new account for another one of my profiles, I found it a bit pushier. They are trying to extend the use of the platform, from statistics and basic information to a friendlier and more holistic approach and want to know your likes, dislikes, hobbies etc. so they can 'helpfully' send you more information in emails and posts. I much preferred the basic 'this is what I do' application, where it provided information on followers and following. I have enough emails already from different platforms without adding another layer.

By using this application on a regular basis (weekly will do), you can build a following faster and cut down on the people who do not follow you and those 'fake' accounts I mentioned earlier. If they don't have an image or sound kosher, then be hesitant about following them.

Helpful links

Crowdfire Review

G2Crowd CrowdFire Reviews

Crowdfire Overview

BoardBooster: Pinterest is a great place to find information and also to post about your books. Boardbooster can help to highlight particular boards and pin new pins to keep it active, even while you are sleeping.

Depending on how much you want to invest in Pinterest as an active social media platform, will determine which Boardbooster package you sign up for. I have the free package, which allows 100 pins per month to be selected or pinned through Boardbooster. You can still do other pinning yourself. To support the free package I also use someone from Fiverr.com on a regular basis to go in and check that I am still visible. I stay away from Pinterest as much as possible, but only because I waste too much time on there.

The top package on Boardbooster is only $50 a month and that is for 5000 pins. If you are an active fan of Pinterest, then I would suggest that Boardbooster is for you.

Helpful links

Boardbooster pricing

A Review of a 4 week Boardbooster

A 7 Day Trial review of Boardbooster

Tailwind is another management tool for Pinterest.

Tailwind v Boardbooster

Crowd Speaking Platforms on Social Media

Over the past few years, there have been many start-ups to encourage further interaction across the internet and social media platforms. One idea seems to have worked really well and is used for many new ventures, as well as authors to gain visibility for their books.

Crowd speaking platforms were created to help users spread a message very quickly, by getting as many people involved with the launch as possible. The idea is to sign up with a project and give a target of how many people you want to try to get involved and set a date/time for the launch. You then advertise your release/launch event and appeal to others for help. They will share the message across their social media platforms, all at the same time. So you flood the market with your message and hopefully, more people will see it and respond.

There are two main contenders for Crowd Speaking platforms, the most popular being Thunderclap and the other being HeadTalker, although there are a few others trying to muscle in on the market. These new ventures are struggling to gain a foothold.

Thunderclap

I really like their introduction 'If a tweet falls in the forest...'

Basically, they are saying that there are so many messages out there, yours may never be seen or heard, but with thousands of people all shouting the same message at the same time, you will get much better visibility and 'noise'.

It doesn't cost anyone anything to sign up and support your message, only maybe a minute of their time. It is easy to help other authors to spread the word about their book and then they could help you. You could also use Thunderclap to raise funds for a project or to link it to an awareness campaign using a hashtag. Check their examples on the 'how it works' link below.

The first time I set up a Thunderclap, I did get a little confused, because you are setting up two promotions at once. One is the main promotion, the cause, the book, the reason; the other is the appeal for friends, colleagues, readers, in fact, anyone, to help spread the word by signing up.

The good thing about Thunderclap (launched in 2012), is that you do not need a huge following on any of your social media platforms to make it work. You need others to sign up, and the message that is sent out on the 'thunderclap' will be sent to all their followers or friends as well as yours, so the more who sign up, the bigger the thunderclap ripple and noise.

All you need to do is have a message that needs sharing, set a goal and date and then send out an appeal. You need to be realistic about your goal because the Thunderclap only happens if you reach your target. There are choices to help.

I would say it's definitely worth it to get some visibility for free. There are packages that can be paid for, especially if you are in a hurry, or want the extras, but give yourself time and everything is free.

Helpful links

Thunderclap and How it Works
5 Things to help your Thunderclap

Allyson R. Abbott & Donna Wolz

6 things you should know before using Thunderclap

Analysis of a Thunderclap Campaign

How to Navigate the Social Media Maze

HeadTalker

Headtalker is really the only alternative to Thunderclap and is gaining ground on Thunderclap. HeadTalker has strong links with the already established HeadFunder, a crowdfunding site and seems to be a natural move for users of that site to use HeadTalker to promote their funding projects and more.

It works in the same way as Thunderclap, where you create your campaign, set targets and dates and then share with as many people as you can. It is free to use and you even get the option to change your end date if you need to find more supporters.

Helpful links

HeadTalker, How it Works
Thunderclap v HeadTalker

Helpful Links to other Other Crowdsourcing Platforms

https://www.daycause.com/t/authors-books
https://guestcrew.com/
https://www.weeral.it/

Allyson R. Abbott & Donna Wolz

Section 7:
Promotional Activities

So far we have given you general information on Social Media platforms and how to use them to your best advantage. Now that you have all that information, let's talk about Promotional Activities and tips for book promotion. This section will cover a lot of the promotional activities that you can do with Facebook, and a lot of these can be extended into G+, Twitter, LinkedIn, Instagram, and Pinterest etc., by posting or tweeting the appropriate information with a link back to the main page. Later in this section, other promotional activities are mentioned and helpful links are provided.

Facebook Promotions

I mentioned some common Promotional Activities when I discussed Facebook. You may know about some, or all of them. You may have participated in some of these activities or organized one. Wherever you are on the spectrum of knowledge, take whatever you want from this information and adapt it to your own needs. You can ask for help on our FB page if you get stuck.

You want to promote every aspect of your book. You can promote cover reveals, book releases, book birthdays, finishing a series, starting a new series, being involved in an anthology, breaking into the top 100, etc. Most of the promotional activities I'll be talking about in this first section will be used for these types of one-time book events.

Don't forget that you also need to be promoting your books on a regular basis after they are released. I'll talk about that farther along in this section.

How to Navigate the Social Media Maze

First, these words from Allyson:

As a newbie, the thought of participating in a takeover or event was a bit scary. I often dropped into them as a reader, but I had no idea how to tackle them as an author. Eventually I took the plunge and signed up to one on a PR event page in which a friend of mine was participating. I didn't really think about it until a day or two before and then casually asked her what I needed to do to prepare. I was very apprehensive about the whole thing.

I'm so glad I asked the question though. I had no idea I needed to plan my time with such precision and to have special banners or images to post as I went along. I am giving you access to my time sheet HERE and some of the images, just so you can see an example, it really did help me.

The other tip, that helped me, if not a little late, was after the event. I had held a few giveaways and the participants needed to comment under my post. It was a 24-hour event and I was one of the first up. Well, you can imagine how many posts there were with at least eight or nine posts per author! The following day I spent ages scrolling through the event page trying to find my giveaway posts to select winners. What I now

How to Navigate the Social Media Maze

know is that, when you post a giveaway, the best thing to do is to click on the top right corner of the post and 'save' the post. By doing this, you can click on 'Saved' in the left-hand column of your Facebook Home page under Explore, and the posts will appear all in a nice list. Hmmm, I wish I had known that before my hours of checking!

I very often use that now when I find a post of interest but don't have time to look into it immediately, so it is useful knowledge for a lot of things.

Okay, let's look at Promotional Activities on FB.

Facebook Event/Party/Takeover:

These can be held on your author page, an event page you create, or with the help of a PR group or FB group. How long they last depends on what you plan to do during the FB Event/Party/Takeover. I will simply call it Event from here on out.

An event can be done different ways.

- You can be the only author featured.
- Multiple authors participate with each one having a designated time slot, typically 30-60 minutes.
- Multiple authors participate by 'dropping in' several times during the event.
- Multiple authors participate in one shared time slot with different time slots occurring throughout the event.

What goes on during a Facebook Event, Party or Takeover?

Anything you want! The purpose of an event is to engage with readers, so however you want to do that is fine. Typically, authors chat with readers about their books, ask and answer questions, give insight into their books, play games, and offer prizes. Anything to keep the participants entertained and interacting.

Games

What kind of games can you play? There is no end to the possibilities! A few suggestions are:

- Ask them to post pictures of something related to your books or associated with you. Tell them what you want them to post: their pet, favorite cover model, best place to vacation, etc.
- Ask them to fill-in-the-blank of a sentence. 'I once ran naked through the ___.' 'I would love to have a date with___.' 'A real friend would never say___.'
- Send them on a treasure hunt. Post a list of items relating to your book and tell them to post pictures of each item.

- Name games. These can be found by searching the internet. Or if you're really creative, make your own.
- Ask them to post **memes** on a certain topic.
- Ask them inane questions and share your own answer.

These are just a few of the limitless games you can play. If you search online, you can find games. Pinterest is a good place to search for games. You can always ask for suggestions for games when you advertise the event.

Prizes

You will need to have prizes to give away. The number of prizes is up to you. The longer the event, the more prizes given away is the norm. You can use some of the games you play as a way to enter the drawings. Prizes can be anything:

- Ebooks
- Paperbacks, signed or unsigned
- Swag, or book related items (for example, your book is called Death by Chocolate, give away chocolate)
- Gift cards
- Whatever you decide.

If multiple authors are participating, they are responsible for having prizes to give away during their time participating in the event.

You need to determine how long you want the Giveaways to stay open. Some close their giveaways at the end of their time slot. Others leave them open a few hours or until the next day. In my opinion, it is best to decide on how you want it done and let all participants know beforehand.

Allyson R. Abbott & Donna Wolz

How to plan a Facebook Event, Party or Takeover

Hosted by a PR Group or FB Group

Let's start with an event hosted by a promotional group like Wise Owls PR. If you want to hire someone or a company to host the event, you don't have to do much to set it up. They also us book bloggers as well as FB book blogs

Here are a few other PRs who may help:

Itsy Bitsy Book Bits Promotions or email Colleen at Itsybitsybookbitspromotions@gmail.com and tell her Allyson sent you.

Lady Amber

There are a lot more out there to choose from and we will collate a long list for the website. HERE

Contact a PR group (we have a huge list for you to look through). Give them a name for the event if you have decided on one. Tell them the date and time and any details they may ask for. They will probably request a media kit (Refer back to Section 1) for the book(s) you are planning to spotlight. Discuss the cost. Once you have agreed on a price, you're done. They will take care of everything else. All you need to do is promote the event on your SM pages and pay them once the event is over.

The PR group will take care of creating the event page and any needed graphics, contacting authors to join the event, organizing everything, and promoting it. Make sure they keep you updated as to what is happening.

An event hosted by a Facebook group is the same as one hosted by a PR group except for a couple of things. If you contact a group, they may or may not request payment. You may be responsible for creating event images or doing other things they ask of you, especially if they are doing it for free. Remember, it is nice to reward those who do it for free with a copy of your book, a gift card, or something else.

If you end up doing more work, why use a Facebook group instead of a PR group? Well, most do it for free and they do most of the work. Secondly, they are there to help if you have questions. Third, they probably have a large following and have experience getting people to attend events. If you're a newbie, you may not have many followers or experience yet.

That being said, if you are paying for an event, always ask for references and then take the time to actually talk with those references. Also ask for an emergency contact. If you are not receiving updates, and no one responds to your inquiries, try to get in touch with the emergency contact. If you are still ignored, send them a note canceling the event and find another PR, or FB, group to host your event. While the vast majority of the PR and FB Groups are legitimate, there are a few unscrupulous people who will take your money and then do nothing, which is why you pay after the event.

Several authors have come to me at the last minute because they hired someone to host an event and nothing was set up. The hosts kept assuring the authors everything was getting organized but refused to give out any information. In one case, it was for a Blog Tour. When the author demanded a list of participating blogs, the host sent her a list. About 80% of the list was inactive or fake blogs. The others were active blogs but they had never been contacted about participating in the tour.

I hear you asking, 'Why didn't the authors contact you in the first place?' The author with the Blog Tour had worked with me in the past and been pleased with my work. She had a new follower who said she did promotional work. The author told me she wanted to give both of us business, which is perfectly okay with me. The other authors I had never worked with, but when they asked for help, Wise Owls PR was recommended.

Events Organized and Hosted by You

You can host the event yourself. There are many reasons to do it yourself:

- It saves money
- You can accept or reject authors who show an interest in participating
- You can make all images to suit your 'vision'
- You determine how to promote the event
- In other words, you have total control

Negatives of hosting an event yourself

- It takes a lot of time
- You have to know how to make images and make them
- You have to keep everything organized
- You have to do all the promoting
- You may not have a large following
- You may not belong to many groups that allow **pimping**
- You have to keep the participating authors up-to-date on what is happening

How to Navigate the Social Media Maze

In other words, you have to do everything yourself.

I didn't mention all the negatives to discourage you. I simply want you to think about all the things you will have to do before you set out to host an event by yourself. I always like to know the pros and cons of anything I plan to do.

What do you need to do to host an event yourself?

Okay, you have decided to host the event yourself. What do you need to do?

- Decide on the reason for the event.
- Name the event: You can decide on a catchy name or go with something simple. For example: Title of your new book Release Day Party or 1000 Likes Celebration.
- You will also need to decide what type of event you want. Will it just be you or are you inviting other authors?
- Is it going to be a drop-in event happening all day?
- Is it going to be a shorter time period with all participation occurring during that time?
- If multi-author, how long are their time slots? 30 or 60 minutes?

- Will you be giving away prizes? Do you expect the other authors to give away prizes?
- Will there be a Grand Prize? If there is a Grand Prize, my advice is to make participation in the event a requirement.
- Are you willing to mail prizes overseas? This needs to be clearly stated in the beginning so readers know.
- How long will the giveaways remain open?
- If you are the only author involved, do you want to do a live video feed?

Decide where you will host the event:

- Your author page
- Your Street Team page
- Your Readers Group page
- Another page you already have
- An event page created just for the event

How to Navigate the Social Media Maze

Create **promotional images** to use for the event. If you don't have access to Photoshop or a similar program to create images, there are sites available for you to use. I use PiZap for most of my image designs. I also use PicMonkey. Both of these sites are easy to use and can be used for free. I have a subscription to PiZap and it is very reasonably priced. My subscription grants me access to more images, fonts, and other features. There are other sites available but these are the only ones I've tried.

Images need to include the event name, date, time, and location. If multi-author, it is nice to have an image with the participating authors' names and time slots once you get everything set up.

Make an image to use as your FB cover photo, as well. It doesn't have to be identical to the other image you make, but should resemble it so people will know it is your event when they see it. *Remember branding is important.*

They don't have to be identical because there is more room for information on a regular image versus a Facebook cover. Use that to your advantage.

Invitations: If it's a multi-author event, then invite other authors. You can contact authors individually if there are certain authors you want to be involved. If not, then put out general invitations on all your SM sites, including your newsletter.

Promote the event. This is usually the hardest part of setting up an event. How can you promote the event? Post the images you've made everywhere across SM and your newsletter. When you post in FB groups, make sure they allow posts concerning events. You don't want your posts deleted and/or you being kicked out of the group. Ask your followers to share the event.

Be sure to include the following information in your posts: name of event, date and time, link to event, information about event including participating authors, how authors can sign up for the event (if applicable), if there is a Grand Prize, and anything else you feel is pertinent.

You need to promote the event as often as possible in as many places as possible. You also need to start promoting as soon as you have decided to host the event and continue right on up to the morning of the event. Ask your followers to share your posts. If multi-author, encourage the participating authors to promote the event as well. This can be accomplished by providing ready-made posts or links to the posts on your page/event page.

During the Event

If a group is hosting the event, you simply need to show up during your allotted time and engage the participating readers in the ways I mentioned earlier. If it is a multi-author event, interact with the other authors as much as possible.

If you are hosting the event, engage with readers in the same way. If it is multi-author, you will need to introduce each author, interact with them during their time slot, and thank them for participating. You will need to be present for the entire event in order to keep things moving.

Facebook Hop

A Facebook Hop is a lot of fun. It can involve authors, bloggers, PR groups, FB groups, and anyone else who wants to participate. Or it can be limited to just authors, authors of a particular genre, or however you want to do it.

During a Hop, readers go to different pages and enter to win prizes by completing the required tasks. Sometimes there is a Grand Prize but that is optional.

Just like an event, you can hire a PR group, ask an FB group to host, or do it yourself. Unlike an event, a hop doesn't have to be related to your books, although it can be. It can be based around a holiday, season, sport (World Series Facebook Hop), pets, anything you want.

If you want someone else to host the event for you, follow the directions listed under Facebook Event.

How to Navigate the Social Media Maze

Hosting a Facebook Hop

Hosting your own Hop is basically the same as hosting an event. It is actually easier than hosting an event. You need to do the same things I mentioned above, plus a few other things.

Decide if there will be a Grand Prize. If there will be a Grand Prize, what will it be? Will each participant donate an item? Will they each donate money for a Gift Card? Or donate money to buy something big like a Kindle Paperwhite? You need to decide this before you contact anyone to participate because they need to know this information up front.

You need to organize the participants into a Master List with links to their page.

Create a post for all participants to post on their page and tell them when they need to have it posted by. For example: Have the following post live on your FB page at 8 am CDT on Memorial Day. Be sure to include the Master List. Here is an example post:

Allyson R. Abbott & Donna Wolz

☆ ̣.•*¨*★☆ Memorial Day Author & Blog Hop ☆★*¨*•. ̣☆

Welcome to my Hop Stop to celebrate Memorial Day!

I've teamed up with some amazing authors and blogs to share some awesome giveaways with you!

All of us have joined together to create a fantastic

GRAND PRIZE GIVEAWAY!

It includes *(List the prize or prizes)*

Here's what you need to do to enter:

1) Visit each Hop Stop and follow the instructions for entering their giveaway. Hop Stops are open from 8 am to 8 pm CDT on Memorial Day.

2) After every Hop Stop has been entered, you are eligible to enter the Grand Prize Drawing. Hop here and comment on this post: *(Insert link.)*

That's it!! Not so hard, right??

•.☆.• The Giveaway For This Hop Stop •.☆.•

(Each participant will list their prize and state whether their Giveaway is open internationally or only in a certain country. If it is limited to a certain country, they can state whether or not they will substitute a gift card to international entrants.)

•.☆.• To Enter This Hop Stop's Giveaway, Please Do The Following •.☆.•

(Each participant will list what they want readers to do. I've simply listed some examples.)

1) LIKE this page- Required

2) Comment below to show us your support and tag a friend or six!- Required

How to Navigate the Social Media Maze

3) SHARING is caring BUT not required

Once you've done that you can....

•.☆.• #HOP HERE NEXT•.☆.•

(Each participant will insert the name and link of the participant listed below them on the Master List.)

To start at the beginning of the Hop, go here →

(Insert link to your Hop Stop post.)

MASTER LIST → *(Insert link to Master List.)*

You will find a full list of the Hop Stops by following the link.

★ ★ The Grand Prize Giveaway winners will be announced on the event page *(Insert date)* ★ ★

Facebook is not responsible in any way for this Hop or the rewarding of prizes.

Each page is responsible for their own page giveaway and the drawing of their winner.

Author *(Insert your name.)* is only responsible for the administration of the Hop, her own Hop Stop prize and for the Grand Prize.

(Insert Hashtags. Again these are just examples.)

#FBHOP #giveaways #authors #bloggers #bookworld

Remember, the post you make doesn't have to look like the example I gave. You can change it to suit your needs. However, all the information I included does need to be in the post, especially the FB disclaimers. FB policy requires a disclaimer every time a Giveaway is posted.

Once you've got the post made, send it to all the participants. Include the images you've made and links to the main Hop page. Describe the Grand Prize. Encourage them to promote the Hop and to use the FB banner as their cover photo.

Just like with an event, you need to promote the Hop everywhere--- as often as possible, in as many places as possible, starting as soon as possible.

How to Navigate the Social Media Maze

Facebook Post Boost

Facebook boosts are a relatively cheap way to promote your posts of books, sales, Events & Hops, and all other aspects of you and your books. You can boost a post for as little as $1/day.

To do this you can either click the 'boost' option at the bottom of your post (if visible) or do it from your homepage.

On your Home page, at the bottom of the left-hand column, is Create. Click Ads. This page appears: Insert image

Simply click on each section in the left-hand column and follow the simple step-by-step instructions. It only takes a couple of minutes and your ad is ready to go.

However, if you really want to get serious about using FB to promote your books, events, even local events, I cannot recommend enough spending some time on Youtube and finding videos that will help you. Search for: getting the most out of FB ads, or using FB for promotions, anything along those lines and watch a few. They can be fairly long and some presenters do go on a bit, but believe me when I say it's worth it. It can help you drill down on the audience to get the best hits possible if you have the time to do it. Definitely worth it if you are doing a local book signing or a promotion.

Helpful Link to get you started. Once you find one video others will show up.

Using FB Advertising

Events That Occur On FB, Blogs and Twitter

Now let's talk about some activities that occur on Facebook, Twitter, and Blogs.

Blog Tour:

Blog Tours consist of your book being promoted on multiple blogs over a set number of days. Most book bloggers also have a Facebook page and Twitter account. They will post the promotion there as well. So, you get coverage on Blogs, FB, and Twitter in one promotion.

Blog Tours are usually used to promote some aspect of your new book. Pre-order and Book Release are the most common Blog Tours. They can also be used to promote sales, series turned into box sets, book anniversaries, or anything else you want to promote.

These are typically run by a PR group but you can run one yourself. A list of Promotion Organizers will be provided shortly.

The length of a tour depends on your opinion of how long it should run or how much money you can afford to spend (if you hire a PR group). Typically they run 1-2 weeks. Like I mentioned earlier, check out any PR group you hire to make sure they are legitimate.

If you hire a PR group, they will need a media kit. If you are offering ARCs for review, they will need that as well. Other than that, they will handle everything that needs to be done. Like an event, make sure you keep tabs on them, as they should keep you updated on a regular basis.

Hosting Your Own Blog Tour

- Decide on the purpose of the tour (New Release, Pre-order, etc.)
- Decide if you offering ARCs and how you are going to send them.
- Decide if you will be including a Giveaway with the tour.
- Create a sign-up form. I prefer to use Google Forms but use whatever you are comfortable with.

How to Navigate the Social Media Maze

The form should include:

- A description of the reason for the tour.
- The name of the book, genre, and blurb. Number of pages is also a good idea to add.
- Your name.
- The dates of the tour.
- Whether you will be sending the media kit with ready-made posts, HTML, DIY posts, and/or Twitter posts. I always send all of these.
- You also need to include how far in advance you will be sending the media kit. Remember, most bloggers are busy people and need to have time to get the post ready for their blog. They can always use the scheduling tool if they get it too early. I recommend sending the information at least a week before the tour starts.
- Whether ARCs are available to review, and when they will be sent out. If the book is part of a series, duet, or trilogy are you offering ARCs of the previous books?

You need to have them provide:

- Contact name
- email address
- Name and URL of blog
- URL to their Facebook page
- URL to Twitter account (Optional)
- 1st and 2nd choices of dates to participate
- Whether they want to review and the Kindle address to send ARCs
- Agreement to not share the ARC with anyone.
- Agreement to post their review on AZ by the date designated.

That was the easy part. Now you have to contact the blogs asking them to participate in the tour. We've helped make this task a little easier by providing you with a massive list of blogs that may be able to help you. If you have a book blog and would like it added to the list then please contact me at
Allyson.abbott@hotmail.com

List of blogs HERE

How to Navigate the Social Media Maze

However, you still have a lot of work to do.

You need to go to the blog sites and determine what type of books they promote. Some blogs promote all genres while others only promote certain genres. Read about the blog and find out how they prefer to be contacted. If they have a submission form, fill it out. If they want you to send your request by email, make note of the name of the blog, contact name, and the email address.

Once you have a list of blogs to contact by email, compose an email inviting them to participate. You can send an email to all the blogs at the same time (Be sure to put the addresses under BCC--blind carbon copy--so everyone's email address is not on display.) or to each blog individually. If you plan on sending to each blog individually, make some notes about the blogs when you are doing your research. Then use that information in the email to add a personal touch.

Either way, you can write a general email with details about yourself (debut author, indie author, etc.), the book, the tour, and the link to the sign-up form. If you send the invitations individually you can leave that part the same for all blogs and then personalize them.

Remember, always be polite, let them know you understand they are busy, and how much it would mean to you to have their support.

If you don't get many positive responses, don't be discouraged. It isn't anything personal. Contact the blogs that didn't respond. I can tell you from experience that sometimes requests aren't answered simply because they arrived on a day when the inbox was flooded with requests, or I had personal issues that took me away from doing anything with the blog, or I was on vacation and the email got lost in my overloaded inbox before my return, and sometimes, I just never got the email for whatever reason.

You can also go back to the list of bloggers and do more research so you can send out more inquiries. This is a good idea even if you got a decent number of responses.

How to Navigate the Social Media Maze

Now you need to get the information organized and ready to send out to the blogs to post on their day of promoting.

To create a packet for a tour, the first thing you need to do is create images. You need a Tour banner and teasers, plus the book cover. You already have the cover and you may already have teasers. That is terrific. You only need to make a Tour banner. There are numerous sites to create images but if you don't know how to do it, there are many places to find someone to make them for you. I design images through Wise Owls PR.

Next, you need to gather the blurb, buy links, excerpt (optional), author bio and picture, plus your Social Media links. Decide on hashtags to use. Once you have everything together, organize the information into a post to send to the participating blogs. Click Here for an example of a post for a tour.

Once you've made the post, you need to convert it to HTML. How to create HTML was discussed in the Blogger part of Section 3.

Send both HTML and the regular post to the blogs.

You may wonder why you need to create the packet in HTML. The reason is most blogs won't agree to participate if HTML is not included.

Create some FB and Twibookbubtter posts to go with this packet.

You will send all this information to the email address they provided on the sign-up form. In addition to the ready-made post, HTML, FB and Twitter posts, you need to attach all the images and the rest of the information so the blog can make their own post if they want to do so.

In the email, thank them for helping you, include a schedule of the dates each blog is supposed to post, and let them know what time you want them to post (Ex. Please have your post live no later than 10 am CDT on the date you are scheduled to post.). Ask them to email you the link to their blog post. Or send the link to a form they need to fill out with their information and links. This will allow you to respond to their posts. To increase the chances each blog will provide their links, have a Giveaway for those that do. Let them know about the Giveaway in the email you send.

Remind the ones reviewing to post their reviews on AZ and add the buy links so it is fast and easy for them to find the book. You can also ask them if they would please post their review on GR and any other site the book is being sold. Again, provide links and ask them to provide you with the URLs to their reviews.

One last thing to include in the email is ask them to tag you whenever they post on FB and Twitter. By tagging, you will get a Notification of each post.

One last thing to keep in mind, not every blog who signed up will post as promised. Not every blog that agreed to review will leave a review. There are many reasons. It is perfectly acceptable to contact them with a gentle reminder. If they still don't post, or let you know what the problem is, remove them from your list of bloggers. There are plenty of bloggers to take their place.

Respond with a Thank You to every blogger that sends you links. By showing your appreciation, they are more likely to help you in the future.

Have I completely scared you out of hosting your own Blog Tour? It can look overwhelming when everything is laid out like that. I assure you, it isn't really as bad as it looks. Just take it one step at a time. If you want to host the tour yourself but need a little help, there are people who will help. I would be happy to create a sign-up form and/or create the post and HTML for a fraction of what it costs to host the tour. I am sure others would be willing to do that as well. Keep that in mind as a way to host the tour yourself without having to do all the work or spend a lot of money.

How to Navigate the Social Media Maze

Blitz

A Blitz is like a Blog Tour except it typically lasts one day. A Blitz is good to promote a Cover Reveal, Book Release, Book Anniversary, Sale, or just to give your book a boost after it has been published.

Blitzes don't typically include getting book reviews but otherwise, they are like a tour. You can hire a PR group or host your own. To host your own, follow the same steps I discussed above. You won't need to offer blogs a choice of dates or ARCs for reviewing. Since they occur on one day, it is much easier to organize because you don't need to determine how to schedule the blogs so each day is covered.

From Allyson: If you have the money in your budget, then I would suggest you pay someone who already has lists of bloggers signed up. By using an organizer with established lists of bloggers or email subscribers, it takes the pain out of having to research blogs and contacting them. They do it all for you.

Of course it all comes at a cost but the balance between cost and time is usually a huge factor. If you only have one book and lots of time, then try doing it yourself, and keep all the information ready for the next time. If you are already into the next book or have a few books to promote, then having an expert and their reach is a much better system.

Other Paid Promotion Opportunities

We have already mentioned blog tours with Facebook and given a list of organizers to help you if you do not want to organize it yourself. There are other ways to pay to promote your book. There are hundreds of promotional businesses and websites offering services to promote your books. As Donna stated earlier, be sure to check their references before you pay. The best way to choose a good one is through endorsement from other authors.

What are these other promotions?

They can be from:

- Established Tweeters with thousands of followers
- Established book promotion companies with thousands of followers and email subscribers
- Established book promoters / bloggers, with hundreds or thousands of followers and subscribers, who offer more than blog tours as promotional activities.

Promoters don't have to have numerous followers to provide good exposure. For example Blog Tours simply need to be able to contact a large # of blogs who will promote.

You can pay $10 for a few regular tweets, to a few hundred dollars for newsletter promotions or perhaps a month long blog tour or blitz. These tours, blitz or blasts may also include Facebook groups or pages but are not exclusive to social media. Whatever you use, it is an investment and you need to invest wisely.

Some promotional platforms have criteria that need to be fulfilled before your book will be accepted; like the length, rating or have so many reviews. Others will only allow certain prices or genres, so you need to check the guidelines for each platform carefully before choosing.

Although BookBub is a fantastic one to promote through and you may get lots of downloads of your book, their selection criteria are extremely narrow and they are costly. However, I have only ever heard good things about them.

How to Navigate the Social Media Maze

The book promoters all offer similar services, but some specialize in certain areas. Again check what they do, compare prices and how many subscribers they have.

- Blog tours, takeovers, release day blasts, cover reveal tours, I have even seen a Title reveal tour!

- Inclusion in an emailed newsletter to their subscribers. These are extremely popular and you can get significant downloads with the right one.

- Inclusion on a website or listing on a page; check to see if it is for a limited period or a lifetime listing. The more places your book is listed the better it is for Google to find it.

- Tweets or other social media posts etc. If they have thousands more followers compared to you, then it is worth trying it out. They can be as little as $30 for a month of daily tweets.

I (Allyson) have some 'go-to' people / book promoters, who will do a good job and deliver what they promise.

These are for services that can include social media but also aim for blog sites (blogger/ WordPress/websites) and direct emails to book lovers. They have access to thousands of more readers and book lovers than I do, so it makes sense to pay for their services.

I don't mind recommending the main services that I use as I know they are good, but don't forget we all may get different results.

Itsy Bitsy Book Bits Promotions or email Colleen at Itsybitsybookbitspromotions@gmail.com and tell her Allyson sent you. They do tours, blitz, blasts, reviews tours takeovers, and book reading services.

Lady Amber : tours for releases, promo's, thunderclap support, and reviews

Books On Fire: tours, cover reveals, sales boosts and lots more

BKnights : costs from $5 for one promotion but has 1000's of followers.

How to Navigate the Social Media Maze

Fussy Librarian : has 120K subscribers to daily emails

Ereader News Today : claim to have 500,000 Facebook followers and nearly 200,000 email subscribers and they do get results.

Book Tweeters : claim 535k+ followers and from $15 will tweet 24 times in 1 day. (other packages available)

Digital Book Today : charge from $10 have impressive amount of following and clicks to Amazon through their email subscribers. I have had good results in the past

The above list just scratched the surface. We have a huge list of PR Contacts for you to look through to save you time. Just click HERE.

If it is only Tweets you are interested these links are a good place to start.

Ask David (@book_tribe)
Goddessfish book promotions

Book Tweeters

Sociaboost

Tweet your Books

For more advice on promotions please check these.

Helpful links

Author Bytes: Social Media Consultation for Authors

Smith Publicity Launch Service

GhostTweeting service to promote you and your book
:Prices visible

Cameron Publicity and Marketing for Authors

WebpageFX Professional Social media Services   has visible pricing and plans

Best Social media Marketing Services

Book marketing

https://www.buzzbundle.com/

/how-to-market-your-book

101-book-marketing-ideas-promote-book/

How to Navigate the Social Media Maze

Promoting Your Books On A Regular Basis

You need to promote your books on a regular basis. If you only promote them through big Promotional Activities, people will forget about them. You can't keep selling to the ones who have already read the book. You always need to work on growing your followers/readers in order to attract more people to buy your books.

How do you do this? By regularly sharing your books on your author page, Street Team page, and any other page you have. You need to be posting in all those FB groups I encouraged you to join. Share across all your SM sites. Get your Street Team involved. Get your followers involved.

While you won't be changing your book covers (you may but not just for sharing), it is a good idea to come up with new teasers to attract attention. New images will keep your book fresh and appealing. Having multiple teaser images will also allow different snippets from your book to be seen. While one teaser might not have piqued a person's interest, a different snippet may cause them to check out your book and buy it.

From Allyson:

As an aside for a moment, I tend to use banners/images to promote in FB groups, but occasionally I use the Amazon sales link within the post to direct possible sales. Using the link very helpfully places the image of my book, with the first few lines of the blurb and also how many reviews or the rating I have for the book. Of course, those statistics change. I garner more reviews and the star rating can change, depending on those reviews. FB, and other sites, remember the data from previous postings and will use the old information unless you tell it not to.

There is a program (free to use on the internet) called [Facebook debugger](#) and if you paste the URL link that has the old data attached, it will replace it with the new data. Very handy to know!

A Wrap-Up of Promotional Activities

In summary, you need to use different types of Promotional Activities to promote your books. Each one I discussed gets your books seen by different people. Multi-author Events and Hops will bring followers of each author to the Event and will expose your books to their readers and vice-versa. Blog Tours and Blitzes will expose your books to followers of the blogs. By sharing your books in multiple FB groups, their followers will see your books. If you only post to your pages you are limiting your exposure.

How else can I promote my books or gain followers?

Newsletters

Normally I am one step behind modern trends. I have never been one to follow fashion or to try and keep up with the new looks, so why should it be any different in my work life? Except that I really should focus on what is happening more and keep up to date with media trends.

One of the best ways of selling books, or so I am told, is to build a **fan-base**. To gather up email addresses of readers interested in your book and send them emails or newsletters when you have a book coming out, or progress on a new book or a giveaway or just some news about your cat. You need to make a connection between you and the readers. You get readers to subscribe to your **newsletter** or regular emails and hopefully they become your fans. I have joined this bandwagon a bit late in the day and am still working on it, hence the invites to sign up for my newsletters.

How to Navigate the Social Media Maze

I have been working on building my email list over the past couple of months, trying to get a bit more visibility. The approach I used was to get involved in multi-author giveaways, blog hops, and other activities through Facebook. This way I was not actually using the direct approach, but blended in as a group. I felt more comfortable, but now realize a lot of participants only sign up to enter the giveaway.

The multi-author giveaways cost between $3 to $25 (depending on if you are offering other prizes and expectations of results), and a commitment to help promote the event. I offered a variety of prizes, including ebooks, a paperback book, CDs, Sun hats, beach bags and gift vouchers. I tried to keep the total prize limit to under $25 for each event. In one event I received a list of over two thousand email subscribers, which sounds brilliant, but as mentioned, I expect a lot of those to unsubscribe when I send out my first newsletter. However, if I get to keep ten percent, then that is twenty more people than I had before and then it may, just may, lead to one or two more book sales.

A lot of interaction for a few book sales, you might think, but then this is the game we all end up playing. You do what you can to promote your book and to find readers and fans. If it doesn't work, then try something else. Plan, do, review, is my mantra. I try lots of different things, if they work, then that is good, if not I tweak it or change tack.

Now, I am going to ask you to sign up to my newsletter [HERE](). By signing up for my newsletter, you will be notified when the next book in the 'Calling All Authors' series, 'How To Navigate the Road to Building Reviews', is released. Whether it is a free book, a giveaway, or even a chapter in the next book in the series, if you can hook readers to sign up, then do it.

After two of these giveaway events I now have 3-4k followers and send out 4 different monthly newsletters aimed at different markets, fiction and nonfiction readers, one for authors, who may be interested in Paragon Book Award events, and then one for Aspiring Authors, who may want to know about events on our Author promotion and Services Facebook page. (Click [here]() if you are interested)

How to Navigate the Social Media Maze

I give people a choice of signing up for one or all, whichever they prefer and I don't always send newsletters each month, only when I have something to say. There is nothing worse than receiving pointless emails. To fill up someone's inbox with rubbish is a quick and easy reason for them to unsubscribe.

I have to admit that I still don't have the time to do all the work for the newsletters, so I contract the job out to a very competent woman named Charity. You can find out more about her and her services at her website HERE.

Each month I outline any information that I would like to send out. I have created an account at Mailchimp and shared the log-in details with Charity. You are allowed to give someone admin rights, so this is all okay.

There are other newsletter and subscriber management systems like Mailerlite and Hubspot and SendinBlue for example and you really need to decide what you want the system to do and how much you want to spend.

Here is a helpful link that compares a lot of the available programs

The Best Emailing Software 2017

I chose Mailchimp because of the free account and Charity is comfortable using it and knowledgeable with its functions.

We designed the newsletter headers between us and before sending out each letter, Charity will send me a copy to check. Her rates are very reasonable and it cuts down on a lot of work, especially if you are trying to focus on writing your next bestselling novel.

Mailchimp does take a while to learn, and they have helpful videos and support. It is a fairly easy site to use, once you know the ropes, but I don't think it is that user-friendly. I would suggest giving yourself a good day or two to go through all the elements and to send a test newsletter to some friends to try it out. Have a few tabs open so you can keep checking the help pages.

They offer a free account if you have up to 2000 registered subscribers, over this number they start to charge. See their price structure. However, there is no reason why you cannot open up another account, with another email address and use that for the overflow. Especially if, like me, you have different newsletters for different readers.

As a point of interest, if you have an Outlook account, it is easy to create a new/additional email address within your account and have all emails coming into the same account.

To create a new email address:

Go to the cog (top right) and click

>options

>Mail

>Accounts

>Connect Accounts (you may need to log in again here to confirm ownership of account)

At the bottom of this page you will find Email Aliases. If you click on that you can make a new email address, that is linked to your account, without having to put in lots of details.

It may also be possible to do the same on Gmail.

Having this option certainly helps. Plus, this is helpful if you want to try a new program or sign up for something without compromising your regular email address. It is also handy if you want to support your fellow authors by signing up to newsletters, but wish to keep them from clogging up your inbox. I keep my inbox very tidy and direct a lot of emails straight to specific inboxes and only check in on them once a day.

Newsletters are a good way to keep in touch with fans and followers who are more likely to buy your latest book, which is why the turnover sales rate is a lot higher than other promotional methods. You can email your fans directly from your regular email provider, but they get very twitchy about hundreds of the same email going out and it could be stopped if it looks like spam.

There are email programs other than MailChimp, but Mailchimp is the biggest and the most used. I believe the '2000' free subscribers is also the highest before any payments are required.

How to Navigate the Social Media Maze

Helpful links

Tips on crafting a popular newsletter

Newsletters for Authors: Get Started Guide

7 steps to effective newsletters

BookBub

Just as I got on the 'newsletter' bandwagon and started to come to grips with regular send outs, gaining followers and interacting with loyal readers, I noticed that a lot of authors are now trying to build followers through BookBub. This is now the new trend and for good reason.

Having followers at BookBub is as good as having a newsletter being sent out with up to date information about new releases, price reductions, etc. They send out relevant information to all your followers in a very timely manner, and not only that, they send you an email letting you know what they are doing. BookBub has a huge following and their promotional events are extremely sought after by authors (although they are very pricey). Being accepted by them for a promotion is a newsworthy event in itself, and will attract hundreds of downloads for your book. It probably will not cover the cost of the promotion, but in the long run, with the increased visibility, it is worth it.

Having your personal 'news' being sent out on a regular basis by BookBub will also help keep your name fresh in the readers' minds, which is never a bad thing.

Amazon

Amazon also has a 'follow' the author program and to some extent helps to promote your books to followers and previous buyers of your books. My personal niggle is that as an author, we have no idea how many followers we have on AZ, although with BookBub it clearly shows you, so it's an incentive to increase the numbers.

With both platforms, the author has no idea who the followers are and cannot contact them directly, so we do need to rely on BookBub and AZ to keep the followers informed. Just think about how powerful these platforms would be if they allowed newsletter creation or a direct messaging system for you to send to your personal followers. It would negate the need for having a newsletter. Especially BookBub, because they would be able to cope with other sales platforms, and not just AZ links.

If I was a betting person, I would suggest that this may be a future development, especially with BookBub, and because of this, I am now trying to increase my following there. I suggest that you get a presence on there and try to get follows. You can create an author page and display all your books. If you want to use them to promote your books, I think you have more chance if you have a large following and sell on different platforms and not just Amazon.

Amazon Giveaways

As far as Amazon is concerned, they also have a promotion program, where anyone can choose a product and create a giveaway. To enter the giveaway you set the criteria i.e., watch a video, follow on Twitter, visit a website, or follow you on AZ.

I very often do a giveaway for one of my paperback books (you pay upfront for the books and basic postage) and request follows at Amazon. Because of the way I have set it up, and the number of giveaways I have done, I know I have thousands of followers. Of course, they can unfollow, or delete the email when they receive the first one, but by then they have had the message and seen my name again. If I do 1-3 giveaways a year, it keeps my follows topped up, my name out there and my books more visible. Each giveaway costs about $20 (2 books and postage), which is fairly cheap publicity.

How to Navigate the Social Media Maze

Twitter ads

You can place ads on Twitter to promote your books, gain followers, or whatever you decide. The cost is very reasonable because what you pay is determined by the amount of interaction your ad receives. For more information, click Here.

Giveaways

I have frequently mentioned Giveaways in this book. Giveaways are used for different purposes but are basically used to draw attention to you and your books. Giveaways are all about building a rapport with readers and gaining new followers.

From Allyson:

Using giveaways to connect with readers through events is a lot of fun. I have taken part in some events on Facebook where you ask fun questions, chat with readers, post quizzes, and then you choose a winner. Interacting with participants helps to build relationships and confidence; it bridges a gap and builds your network. If you have been chatting with someone for a while on Facebook, you are more likely to remember that person down the line, when you have another book that needs a review, or you want an opinion on the cover, or something else, so you reach out to them for help. These small interactions build friends, fans, and readers of your books. It makes you approachable and builds a personality for your face.

What kind of items can be used for Giveaways? Prizes can be anything: ebooks, paperbacks, swag, book related items (for example, if your book is called Hawaiian Shenanigans, you might give away beach related items), gift cards, ereaders, subscriptions to KU or other book-related subscriptions. There are no limits on what you can use for prizes.

Over the past couple of years, I have received a wide variety of items. For example: numerous signed paperbacks (which I really love) and ebooks; gift cards, pens, bookmarks, key chains, mugs, coffee and tea, a wine glass, wine charms, Godiva chocolate, t-shirts, tote bags, a beach bag, a beach towel, a Kindle Fire, stuffed animals (a dragon, cat, unicorn, horse) and much more. As you can see, the only limit to what you can give as prizes is your imagination and budget.

How to Navigate the Social Media Maze

Often, multi-author Promotional Activities give away a Grand Prize. All participating authors contribute a few dollars and the prize is something big like a Kindle ereader or $100 PayPal cash or a gift card.

Giveaways included in Promotional Activities draw attention to the activity. By adding a Giveaway you are likely to gain more buzz for your event, but it also begs the question: Are people who enter your giveaway doing so because they are readers and interested in your book, or just want the prize? Either way, your event will be noticed by more people, and sometimes it is a matter of getting your name recognized, and not always about sales.

You can run a Giveaway on any of your Facebook pages. Simply make a post describing what is required to enter and what the Prize will be. Include when the Giveaway will end. Facebook requires a disclaimer stating they are not involved in the contest. For example: FB is in no way responsible for this Giveaway. I am solely responsible.

You can include contests in your newsletters as well. You can include a link to a Giveaway on your Facebook page, website, a sign-up form, or Rafflecopter. If you prefer, you can ask newsletter subscribers to email you the required information. There are readers who don't have a Facebook account, so it is a good idea to offer them alternative ways to enter.

You can also have Giveaways on Twitter, Goodreads, and LibraryThing.

You can set up a Giveaway using Rafflecopter, which is extremely easy to use.

Helpful link

Take a Tour

This explains how it works and gives you suggestions about what tasks to have entrants perform to gain entries.

When the giveaway is over, Rafflecopter lets you choose a random winner and verify they did the required task(s), and then contact the winner from the giveaway form. You can also announce the winner via Rafflecopter. What could be easier?

It is free to run a Rafflecopter giveaway. That's all I've ever used. However, there is a paid service that allows you to do more things. Prices range from $13-$84 per month. Click Here to read about what the different plans offer.

Helpful links

How to Create a Giveaway Campaign

Choosing a Winner

When you run a Giveaway/Contest you have to pick a winner. How can you pick a winner? Close your eyes and point at the computer screen? Have your friend choose a name from the entries? Choose the person who helps you the most? You could do those things but there are better, unbiased ways to do it.

There are several sites to help you randomly pick a winner. I'm going to mention the two I use.

Random.org

Random.org is a very useful site when picking a Giveaway winner. It allows you to choose a winner at random, eliminating any hint of bias. Trust me when I say you want to be completely unbiased when it comes to picking a winner. The two features I'm going to discuss are completely free to use.

If every entrant in a Giveaway has one entry, you can use the True Random Number Generator. It is found on the right-hand side near the top of the page next to *What's this fuss about true randomness?* Determine the number of entries. Enter that number in the box marked max and click *Generate.* A number will appear in the *Result* box. That is the number of the winner. Count down your list of entrants until you reach that number. You have now chosen a winner completely at random.

If the Giveaway is set up to allow each entrant multiple entries, I prefer to use *List Randomizer.* Scroll down the page until you see *Lists and Strings and Maps, Oh My!* The first option is *List Randomizer*. Enter each entrant's name once for each entry they have. Click *Randomize* and you have picked a winner at random.

There are other features on Random.org for you to use. The ones I mentioned are the only ones I've used.

The Alphabetizer

The Alphabetizer is another site I like to use. It is free, also.

There have been many times I needed to alphabetize a long list or remove duplicates. I can do that, as well as several other things: *Strip HTML, Sort by Last Name, Sort Titles, Make All Lowercase, Capitalize First Word, Reverse List, Ignore Indefinite Articles, Ignore Definite Articles, and Randomize!*

All you do is enter your list of entrants and click *Randomize!*. Another easy way to randomly choose a winner.

A Final Summation of Book Promotions (From Donna)

There are so many ways to promote your books. Which methods should you use? Where are the best places to spend your money? After talking with several authors, I want to share their thoughts on the best ways to promote your books.

Facebook and Twitter are great ways to keep your name and your books in front of readers on a daily basis. They allow authors to connect with readers in a personal way. By asking questions about their reading preferences, where they buy books, prices they pay for books, etc., an author can gain insight into what readers want in books.

The general consensus is building your newsletter subscriber list is extremely important. By having a large number of subscribers, you are basically accomplishing what paid promotion sites do when they send your book details to their subscribers. Your reach may not be as big as the promotion sites' but your subscribers are made aware of your books, sales, giveaways, etc. on a regular basis which leads to name recommendation.

Cross-promoting with authors in your genre allows their followers to learn about your books. Since they enjoy reading that genre there is a good chance they will buy your books. Plus, readers tend to trust the recommendations of authors whose books they read. You can cross-promote on SM sites, newsletters, websites, and in the back of your books.

The following list of promotion sites have a proven track record according to the authors I talked with. The first four are more expensive than the last three but a promotion with them typically produces a decent number of sales as well as sales of other books and reads on KU. The last three offer a decent number of sales for the price.

Freebooksy is a site where you can promote your free books. They can be perma-free or free for a limited time. Your book will be featured on the homepage of their website and sent via email to subscribers interested in that genre. It will be shared on Facebook where they have 245,000+ followers. Costs range from $40 to $200 depending on genre.

Bargain Booksy is affiliated with Free Booksy. It is for books priced 99c to $5.00. Your book will be featured on their website and sent to subscribers via email. Costs range from $25 to $150 depending on genre.

Robin Reads is a site to promote free and 99c books. Positive reviews are required before they will accept your book. Submit your book for review and they will let you know whether or not they will accept it. Costs range from $40 to $80 depending on genre.

Ereader News Today is a site to promote books priced free to $2.99. Positive reviews will help in getting your book accepted for promotion. Just like Robin Reads, they will review your book to determine if they will accept it. Costs range from $35 to $140 depending on genre and price.

The Fussy Librarian is a site to promote books priced $5.99 and less. Your book is featured in their newsletter and appears on their site for 30 days. Costs range from $8 to $18.

eBook Discovery is a site that promotes books from new authors as well as established authors. They offer free and affordable promotion options. Share a post from their FB page and they will reciprocate. Increase the number of subscribers to your newsletter with their Build Your Newsletter promotion. They offer promotions to be in their Daily eZine, to promote series, and to have your own eZine with costs ranging from $25 to $75. You can also submit your books for reviews.

EbookSoda promotes books priced $4.99 and less. Positive reviews are required before they will consider your book. Books are posted on their site and sent in emails to subscribers. A standard listing costs $15. For an extra $6.00, your book will be shared on their FB or Twitter account.

Remember, no single method of book promotion is going to work miracles. Nor is a one-time promotion enough to keep sales coming in. Be prepared to keep promoting your books forever. Use a variety of methods and continue to use the ones that give you the best results. Do whatever is necessary—legally, of course --to keep your name and your books in the public eye.

Swag

It has become part of the author environment to have book-related items to give to readers. These products are known as swag. Swag comes in many different forms like bookmarks, pens, t-shirts, tote bags/drawstring bags, magnets, coasters, mugs, towels, lip balm/gloss, key chains, compacts, mouse pads, water bottles/flasks, and much more. The one thing all swag has in common is that it promotes the author or a particular book through an image or the title/name.

Why do you need swag? Readers enjoy getting items from their favorite authors that are related to the books they love. You can use swag as Giveaway prizes, as rewards for your active Street Team or ARC Team members, as a Thank You to a reader, or any number of reasons. If you attend a Book Signing/Convention, it is good to have swag available to give people who stop by your table. By providing swag, you are putting your name and book covers in front of a large group of people. When people have a visual reminder of your books, they are more likely to take a look at your books on retail sites and thus, more likely to buy your books.

From Allyson,

It can be an expensive venture, but it helps to build on reader connections and your brand. I have never gone down this route for promoting, mainly because I am always on the move, so I rarely have a permanent address for deliveries; also I have (as yet) never attended a book fair. But it can be a lot of fun to have items with your name, your book title or the series, with visuals for emphasis. I recently had hand towels and some book charms created, as a test for a project, and the results were stunning. Donna is looking after them for me and they will be used for a giveaway at a later date. Here are two of my book covers as hand towels and tiny book charms.

It can get costly, but it is part of marketing and publicity.

These items were made for me by Crafty McSwaggerton

I (Donna) recommend Crafty McSwaggerton. She has made numerous items for me and they are all high quality. She doesn't consider an item finished until she is 100% satisfied. I've seen her throw out items that looked fine to me but she wasn't satisfied with a minor detail.

The towels shown above are so soft and plush. The white is so bright making the towels look extra nice. The book charms are small, yet you can still read the writing. They also have actual pages.

Since Allyson has never used swag, or seen the items made by Crafty McSwaggerton, she doesn't feel she can endorse any particular swag maker, which is perfectly understandable.

How to Navigate the Social Media Maze

From Allyson:

I have a few swag web links for you, but please note I am not endorsing them, just giving you a few options. It may be good to ask other authors who they use, or search your followers/friends on Facebook or Twitter and look for swag makers.

Helpful links

https://www.facebook.com/SwagbyNaNa/
https://www.facebook.com/BookSwagNinja/

Book Awards and Competitions

If you are confident your story, cover, and blurb are terrific, then why not enter it into a competition? They usually only cost a few dollars to enter, and a book cover with an award-winning logo on it is extremely attractive to a reader. It spikes more interest. Think about your own reaction to seeing a cover or a book that states it is an Award Winning Book?

Winning, or even being a finalist or shortlisted for a book award, is a great way to get noticed and help with marketing. Some awards can be pricey, but you need to balance that against how well-known they are and what you are entering it for.

To get an emedal for your book, and to say you are an Award Winning Author, will always get you brownie points and more visibility, not just for the book that won, but for all your books. So check these out and think about it. Apart from money, you have nothing to lose.

How to Navigate the Social Media Maze

Helpful links

Aerogramme-Awards/Competitions and courses

Dan Poynter's 2018 Global Ebook Awards

Independent Press Book Awards

The Book Designer Book Awards

Virginia Romance Writers

New Zealand Book Awards Trust

Independent Publisher Awards

Indie Book Awards

Paragon Book Awards and Flash Fiction Competition

Readers' Favorite Award Contest

Best Book Awards

The Bridport Prize

There are also ways to earn money with writing. I have listed a few. Making a name as a regular article writer will undoubtedly highlight all your work.

Writing Jobs: Freedom With Writing

Alaska Airlines Magazine (paid articles)

Allyson R. Abbott & Donna Wolz

Some final words of wisdom

From Allyson:

Being an Indie author does come with many different hats. The promotion hat is the biggest and has the widest brim. It can cover so many elements from posting a tweet, creating a media kit to doing a book signing at a book fair, with hundreds of hours in between trying to keep your books in the public eye.

The more books you write, the more work there is. Even if you decide not to become an independent and look for a publisher (or even a hybrid like me, where two of my books are published through a publisher), you will still need to be active on the promotion front. A lot of publishers will look at your social media platform to see what sort of following you have already. Publishers want to see active authors. They need to see that you have good interaction with followers and know how to use social media. You will have a much better chance of attracting a publishing contract if you have an active social media platform.

How to Navigate the Social Media Maze

Setting out from a cold start is a long haul, but if you have followed our advice and started building your platform as you began to write, you will have a much better foothold when approaching publishers.

Being published or doing it yourself still involves a lot of promotion, so how do you juggle all these tasks.

Here are a few tips

- Decide which social media platforms to sign up for, and limit your choice.
- If you do sign up to more for a broader platform, limit which ones you visit weekly and those you visit each day, or every other day.
- Start to build a Street Team from the get-go, even if initially it's only friends and family members.
- If needed, split the team members into specific tasks (matching the members strengths and abilities)
- Make one or two trusted members of the Street Team supervisors and delegate tasks.
- Learn to trust and delegate. Keep the most personal tasks for yourself.
- Only visit SM platforms for 1-2 hours a day at the most, and choose who and what you

interact with. Logout of social media platforms when writing.

- Decide what your strengths are within promoting. If you are great at creating banners or writing blurbs, then do them. If not, then find a service to do them for you. Your time is better spent writing than struggling learning new tasks.

- Find other authors who you can 'skill swap' with. Recently someone edited my book while I created the cover and my husband formatted her MS. Work to your strengths.

- Cross promote with other authors using blogs, newsletters, or FB pages to become visible to more readers.

- Make a list of the most helpful and best services you find. There are so many choices for promotions via email send outs, blog hops, tours etc., but not all get results. Ask advice from other authors and create a database for future use. Even if you see a recommendation and you don't have a book ready to promote, make a note of the name.

- Use Fiverr.com to find cheap (but make sure they have good feedback) to take over some Pinterest, Instagram, Google+ blog post chores, if you can afford it. Create a temporary password, while others have access.

- Don't think you have to do everything yourself, just because you are an indie author. You will become too embroiled in all the tasks and forget that you have a book that needs writing.

- If possible, create a list of all the places you submitted the book, or the cover image. If further down the line you want to add a medal to the cover, or a bestseller logo, it will save time.

- As you write more books, you will probably be adding earlier books to the back matter of newly published books. Create a folder (on the desktop is easier) to house the covers and blurbs of all your books, this will make it easier to add the information, or to make changes. It makes it easier when you are publishing a new book to have everything in one place.

- Set aside an afternoon or one day each week, when you set up your marketing banners or tweets for the next week, and use a scheduling platform if possible; although you can schedule posts on Facebook directly and also on most blogs.

- Keep up with regular follows/likes to help build your platform. This task could be delegated. But if you do it yourself, only spend fifteen minutes a day. That small amount will help to expand your network.

- If you use Facebook to boost your posts, learn how to focus your target audience for effective promotions.

- Some days you will not get everything done that you hoped you would. Accept the fact that you have off days and try to refocus for the next day. Remember you have a life to live as well.

- Take a break from writing when you are stuck. Even doing the dishes can be lucrative, as it helps your mind to relax and ideas can pop into your head.

- Keep a notebook handy or use your phone to jot down things at odd moments. It will save you from wracking your brain later on when trying to recall that idea.

- Although it is not recommended, I would suggest that you keep the same password for most of the social media accounts, or at least just change the first or last character. You do end up having so many places you need to register on, it is hard to keep track.

I could keep writing tips all day, but most authors need to experience the workload to appreciate the advice. My most used advice is to remember to have fun and enjoy the ride you get from meeting new friends and experiencing the indie author/reader community. You will not find a better place to hang out.

How to Navigate the Social Media Maze

From Donna:

WOW! We have given you so much information to think about. Hopefully, you have gained some knowledge that will help you as you work toward growing your fan base, promoting your books, and garnering sales.

I know it can seem intimidating when you look at the book as a whole. My advice is, don't try to tackle everything at once. Choose one thing and work on that. Then, pick another. If you do one thing at a time, everything will eventually fall in to place.

Some last minute points:

- Using Social Media is a time-consuming endeavor. If you aren't careful, your entire life will revolve solely around SM. It is extremely important to set a limit on how much time you are willing to spend on SM and then stick to it. You need to leave time in your schedule for the really important things: your family, your job, writing, and relaxing.
- Set a budget and stick to it.
- Remember, there are so many people who are willing to help you on your journey as an author. Don't be afraid to ask for advice/guidance or help of any kind.

- Always be on the lookout for new ideas to help you promote your books and yourself. Be creative. Unique approaches will typically pique people's interest.

- Interact with other authors and readers. The more visible you are, the more books you are likely to sell.

- Delegate whenever possible. If you can afford it, hire a PA to free up some of your time.

- BREATHE! If everything doesn't get done, don't fret about it. Re-evaluate your plan and make adjustments.

- Have fun. Using SM to promote your books should be relaxing and enjoyable.

In the next section, you will find the glossary of terms. These are all the words that have been emboldened throughout the book.

I hope you have found this book helpful. Please remember that all reviews are helpful, not only for us but for future readers and authors. Please, when you have time, leave us a review.

With best wishes for your writing career,
All the best from
Allyson R Abbott and Donna Wolz

How to Navigate the Social Media Maze

Find us at the following links:

Allyson R Abbott

http://www.AllysonRAbbott.com

email Allyson.Abbott@hotmail.com

Blog:

http://AllysonRAbbott.blogspot.com

Goodreads:

http://www.goodreads.com/AllysonRAbbott

Facebook:

https://www.facebook.com/AllysonRAbbott

Twitter:

https://twitter.com/AllysonRAbbott

LinkedIn:

http://www.linkedin.com/in/AllysonRAbbott

Allyson R. Abbott & Donna Wolz

Donna Wolz and Wise Owls PR

email:

wiseowlspr@yahoo.com

Facebook:

https://www.facebook.com/donna.wolz

https://www.facebook.com/WiseOwlsPR/

Twitter:

https://twitter.com/WiseOwlsPR

Facebook: Author Promotion & Support with Paragon & Wise Owls PR

https://www.facebook.com/authorpromotionandsupport/

Amazon Author Page:

https://www.amazon.com/Donna-Wolz/e/B075ZBR9BT

GoodReads Author Page:

https://www.goodreads.com/author/show/17191235.Donna_Wolz

Glossary of Terms

Anthology: A published collection of stories written by one author or multiple authors

App/Application: Most people think an App has to do with mobile phones or tablets, whereas an App, which is short for Application, is like an extra tool that can be used, whether on a mobile device or a website. Google Drive has lots of Apps to enhance user experience.

ARC Teams: ARC (Advanced Reader Copy) teams are a group of people who receive an ARC before the book is published in order to review it. They can leave their reviews on GR before the release date. On release day, they post their reviews on the retail sites.

Author Platform: An Author Platform, simply put, is your visibility as an author.

Bitly: You can shorten URL links on Bitly to use on all social media sites. Once you share them you can see traffic and referral links and daily trends. You can also edit, share, or tag the link from Bitly.

Blitz: Like a book tour, but a lot of posts in a short amount of time to help promote your book release, a price reduction etc.

Blog: A website, very often just one page where the owner can post text and images about anything on a regular basis. The aim is usually to gain a following or to keep your followers informed. Blog platforms: Wordpress, Blogger, Tumblr, Ghost, DrupaL and others.

Blog tour: Pre-scheduled virtual tour that interacts with lots of blogs (usually all using the same post) and sticking to a pre-arranged schedule

Bloggers: People who create and write a blog, sometimes a private blog or they can be public and shared with everyone. Lots of book bloggers sign up for virtual book tours

Blurb: A short, catchy description to advertise a book - used as a book description on Amazon—the description on the book jacket or inside flap of a print book.

Book Awards: Are like writing competitions, but encourage you to enter your book (previously written) into a category. Winning, or even becoming a finalist, will probably earn you an e-medal that you can add to your ebook cover. This along with the words 'Award Winning Author' will add kudos to your profile and all your books. ParagonBookAwards.com has a competition for New Authors and is only $25 to enter.

Book blogs: Blogs with a book theme - like book review blogs

BookFunnel: They are a paid service (starting at $20) to help authors to give away free books. If you want to give a book away, you can ask the recipient to go to BookFunnel for a free copy, rather than have to price the book free on a sales platform, or send the book yourself via email. The recipient can choose the format as well.

Book Review tour: A tour where readers sign up to review your book. This doesn't include posting book details. It is simply to get reviews.

BookLinker: Create a link to your Amazon books or your Amazon author page at Booklinker that works on all Amazon international I stores, so you can promote to a global reader base with one link and customize to your book title. For example, clicking on http://myBook.to/EnglishRose will take you to this book on the Amazon store in your country.

Book2Read: is similar to Booklinker, but Book2Read.com has extended links to all sales platforms for that book, so it is not exclusively for Amazon. Check this link: http://Books2Read.com/AKiss1. With Books2Read you can also use any affiliate accounts you may have when creating the links. Book2Read is a D2D service.

Bought promotion opportunities: Sites and services that promote books for authors for a fee. BookBub is the best for ebooks but it is hard to get in and they are rather expensive though the price is worth it. BKnights on fiverr is a good one for free book promotions and sometimes they work well for 99¢ ebooks on Amazon. There are many and before you use any, always ask other authors if they've heard of it or used it and what their experience was before you use any of the paid services.

Competitions (see book awards): Writing competitions give you a chance to win awards to describe yourself as an award winning author. They are usually judged by editors and agents which gives you a chance to get your work seen by them and some of the competitions include publishing contracts. For romance writers, RWA is famous for the different competitions they run yearly.

ConvertKit: A newsletter service built by bloggers, for bloggers, to help you build your business with email marketing.

Cover reveal: A cover reveal is an organized event where you let the world, or at least your followers, see the book cover for your next book.

Cross Promotion: Cross promotion is a form of authors supporting each other through promoting books on each other's blogs, newsletters, or social media sites. You can do interviews with each other. You can promote other authors in the back matter of your book.

CSV File: A CSV is a comma separated values file which allows data to be saved in a table structured format. Typically they take the form of a text file containing information separated by commas, hence the name.

D2D: Draft2Digital. Draft2Digital is a popular self-publishing site that distributes to the big online ebook stores.

Emailed Promotions: Email marketing for your books. Sending emails with info on your books to your reader list to promote your books. There are quite a few websites and promotional businesses to choose from who offer these services, they do cost and there are no guarantees, but probably worth it for the publicity. If the book does not get a lot of downloads then I suggest looking at the cover and blurb and see if they need changing.

Event: A happening to promote your books like a book signing, a presentation, or a book reading

Excerpt: A passage taken from your book, generally used for marketing or promotion to entice readers.

Facebook: An online social networking site where people can create profiles, share information, and respond to the information posted by others.

Facebook Event/Party: An organized event on a specific date and time frame on Facebook to post about your books and interact with readers to promote your books.

Fan Base: Regular supporters and enthusiasts who, hopefully, are waiting for your next release. **Fanfics:** A story written by a fan about the characters and world created by an author

Ficlets: A short story written to be given away as a gift to readers. It is typically 500 to 3000 words and is a bonus scene or extended epilogue to a story.

Fiverr.com: A global online marketplace offering tasks and services, beginning at a cost of $5 per job performed.

Followers: Readers who like/follow you on Social Media, or even some sales platforms; followers may interact with you.

Free books: To give away books for promotional purposes or you might have a permanent free book, like a first book in the series, to entice readers to buy the other books.

Giveaways: To give away one of your books or a prize that readers would like, as a way to draw attention to your book, a way to promote all your books. If it's something you're shipping, specify the country or countries the contest is limited to as overseas delivery is expensive.

Goodreads: A site for book lovers to find books to read and to leave reviews. The website allows individuals to search Goodreads' database of books, annotations, and reviews. Users can create their own groups of book suggestions, surveys, polls, blogs, and discussions.

Google +/G+: is a social networking site run by Google.

Instafreebie: They have a 30 day free trial period to set up a book give away. You can use Instafreebie with MailChimp to entice more subscribers to your newsletter by having them subscribe to get the free book.

Likes: The like button is a feature of social networking service Facebook, where users can like content such as status updates, comments, photos, and links shared by friends. When a user clicks the like button, the content appears in the News Feeds of that user's friends.

Log Line: The log line is a condensed description of a book in 25 words or less. Sometimes used at the top of blurb or sales page.

MailerLite: A newsletter service that lets you easily create great looking email newsletters, manage subscribers, track your results and much more.

Mailchimp: Mailchimp is a newsletter service that helps create newsletters and offers sign up forms for your web page, etc.

Meme: an amusing or interesting item (such as a captioned picture or video) that is spread widely online, especially through social media

Movie Maker: A Microsoft Windows tool that lets you make and edit videos to make book trailers, vlogs, or other videos to post on Youtube.com and other platforms.

MS: Manuscript

Multi-Author Giveaways: where authors come together and each contribute financially and offer gift vouchers, books or other prizes to encourage readers to sign up for newsletters, to follow or like or some other kind of interaction.

Multimedia: Different media platforms that can be utilized for gathering or presenting information. This can be physical, virtual or audio.

Newsletter: A physical, or most often, emailed update of news, information and events. It is seen as very advantageous for authors to build an email list of 'fans' to promote their books to.

Perma free books: Some online ebook sellers (particularly Amazon) do not like books to be permanently free. I can understand that, as they will not make any money from the download, in fact it costs them to download the book to the receiver. However, it is sometimes advantageous for authors to have a book that is permanently free, especially if it is the first book of a series. Some publishers/sales like Draft2Digital, allow permanent free books, as they understand they may benefit from sales of other books in the series. To get Amazon to make an ebook permanently free (perma free), you need to put your book for free on other sites and then get a few people to point out to Amazon that a book they are selling is free elsewhere.

Personal Assistant (PA or VA): A personal or virtual assistant is somebody who works for you and takes over some of the promotional or administrative tasks on a regular basis. They can be either paid or they may be part of your fan club and work for free.

PicMonkey: PicMonkey offers a free plan to edit pictures and graphics and add text to them. Great for making meme's and teasers. User-friendly. You do not need to sign up to use the basic services.

Pimping: Urban slang popular with the indie book community. It denotes promoting in many places, like fans sharing their favorite authors' book info.

Pinterest: A Social Media site that allows you to share images. Images are 'pinned' to 'boards' you create.

Pitch/Elevator pitch: A slang term used to describe a brief speech that outlines an idea for a product, service or project. The name comes from the notion that the speech should be delivered in the short time period of an elevator ride, usually 20-60 seconds.

PiZap: PiZap is a *'Photo Editor, Collage Maker, Design Tool'* that allows you to create custom images to suit your needs. It offers a free version and a paid version. Extremely user-friendly.

PM (Private Message): Confidential way to communicate on SM sites between approved contacts like a chat/texting or in FB's Messenger.

Podcasts: An audio file/broadcast like a radio show on the internet where you can talk about and promote your book or be interviewed about your book.

PR group: A business designed to promote authors across Social Media for a fee.

Pricing: Setting a price for your book, for instance you might choose to promote a book for a low price like 99¢ for a limited time, or for a regular price of $3.99.

Promotion: The advancement of a product, idea, or point of view through publicity and/or advertising.

Rafflecopter: Rafflecopter is a free contest tool. You fill out the required information including what the prize is and what they need to do to enter the contest. For example: *'like'* your Facebook page, or sign up for your newsletter. Rafflecopter takes care of the rest.

Random.org: Random.org is a website that produces random numbers or randomizes lists so you can select the winner of your contest without bias.

Readers' Favorite: On Reader's favorite web site you can receive free book reviews from readers and also they have a book contest each year. Also the Predators and Editors Readers Poll allows readers to vote on their favorite books in several categories with a winner in each category.

Release day: The first day the book is available for sale. Book launch day.

Reviewers: People who write critiques (reviews) of books on websites and other media platforms.

Royalties: A sum of money paid to an author for each copy of a book sold.

SEO: SEO or Search Engine Optimization is the name given to activity that attempts to improve search engine rankings.

Skype: This is a software application that allows users to make voice and video calls over the internet.

SMS: Short Message Service: A system for sending short text messages, as from one cell phone to another or from a computer to a cell phone.

Social Network/Social Media Network: A social network is an online platform which people use to build relations with other people who share similar interests.

Stalkers: Avid fans known to follow their favorite authors across all platforms.

Stalker links: This is a term used in the indie book community to indicate SM links to follow authors across all platforms.

Star rating: Stars are often used as symbols for classification purposes. They are used by book reviewers to help others know if they enjoyed a book or not.

Street Teams: A group of fans who support you by pimping your books. They work for free, but you can reward them with gift cards, swag, free books etc.

Swag: Promotional items to give away to promote your book like book marks, postcards, magnets, keychains, and other items.

Tagging: You can tag someone on FB by putting @ before their name (@your name) and clicking on their name from the list that appears. On Twitter, add their Username (@WiseOwlsPR) to the Tweet. They will get a notification stating someone has 'tagged' them. They can then easily find the comment they were tagged in.

Tag line: A catch phrase about the book that goes on the cover or a general catch phrase you use everywhere as part of your brand.

Takeover: An organized event for a short period of time(usually 30 minutes to 1 hour) in which you post information, blurbs, excerpts, teasers, cover art, etc about your book(s) and interact with the readers who participate.

Teasers: An image with a quote from a book used to entice a reader to buy the book.

Tinyurl: Tinyurl.com is like Bitly, but it only makes a URL smaller - no additional services - but it's free and easy to use.

Trailers: A video about your book using words and images, including lines from your blurb and the cover art with background music. You post it on YouTube.com and other platforms to promote your book.

Troll: A person who enjoys sowing discord on the Internet by starting quarrels or upsetting people, by posting inflammatory or off-topic messages in an online community with the intent of provoking readers into an emotional response or of otherwise disrupting normal, on-topic discussion, often for the troll's amusement. They will give your books 1-star ratings out of spite. They usually run in packs so when one starts harassing you, expect others to follow. Be aware, it is best to ignore trolls or to report them. If your friends or fans try to strike back, especially at Amazon by clicking 'NO' that the troll's review didn't help to decide on the book, then they will cause even more trouble, so it's a vicious cycle and you will lose.

Twitter/Tweet promotions: Using Twitter to promote your book. This can be done by yourself or you can use a paid service.

URL: Uniform Resource Locator is a reference (an address) to a resource on the Internet. It can be found at the top of the page in the address bar.

VerticalResponse: VerticalResponse Email and social media marketing in one place. You can create web pages in conjunction with your newsletter.

Video: A recording of a moving visual image, often with captions and music.

Vlog: Is like a blog, but instead of a written piece of work it is a video post and very often gets posted on YouTube. You could talk about your books or the writing process.

Website: A site on the internet that usually has multiple pages like an about me page, a contact page, pages to post information on your books, etc.

YouTube.com: Used by writers to post book trailers, video recordings of panels you do, interviews you do, or readings of your books or vlogs.

Allyson R. Abbott & Donna Wolz

How to Navigate The Path from Writing to Publishing
A 'Go To' Handbook for Indie Authors!

By Award Winning and International Bestselling Author: Allyson R. Abbott

Calling all Authors…Especially Indie Authors; at last, an easy to understand help book to guide you along the path from Writing to Publishing.

Have you ever wondered about writing and self-publishing? Are you lacking in confidence, because you don't know where to begin, or how to start?

Are you flummoxed by all the jargon and terminology that seems common place on the internet?

Does the thought of self-publishing scare you?

I take you through the whole process, giving advice, explaining the jargon, highlighting good practice and also the pitfalls to watch out for.

This book clarifies the different stages of the writing to publishing process and describes each step from personal experience, backed up with expert advice from linked sources scattered throughout each page.

With a resource webpage on tap with hundreds of extra resource links, this 'go to' handbook is a must for all aspiring and newbie authors or writers, as well as established authors who are looking to take a step from a traditional publisher to begin a new journey as a hybrid author.

Welcome to the learning curve of being and Indie Author, with this book your journey will be made easier.

About Allyson

I'm very lucky to have the indulgence of time and space to enable me to write. I took a sabbatical from work to accompany my partner on his bucket list travels and adventures, and never went back. I really thought I would struggle with all the free time, so decided to write to keep myself occupied. Now writing has consumed my time and I am never sure where we will be or when, hence my novels could be classed 'international' as they may have been written across a few countries. We are still travelling, although we do pop back to the UK for a few months every now and again.

I love the fact that no matter what our age we can use new technology to connect to the rest of the world and enhance our lives. Back in the UK I have my friends and family and with emails, phones, Skype or face-time, we are never out of touch for long. Even my mother at eighty-six uses face-time to catch up with me. I have the world at my fingertips and only twenty-four hours away from anywhere.

Being a 'mature aging gracefully' woman, I feel akin to the problems of aging and relationships. I spent many years on my own before finding my truly remarkable and very patient partner who I happily gave up my whole world for. My stories are about mature relationships with mature people. People who have character and humour, who have a history; people just like us.

I like to call it Hen Lit, Not Chick Lit, but it is not just about falling in love. They are about real relationships.

How to Navigate the Social Media Maze

I hope you enjoy my stories. Please check my web page or social media pages if you would like to contact me. I love emails and try to answer every one as soon as possible.

Allyson R. Abbott & Donna Wolz

About Donna

Donna is a huge animal lover and currently has 3 cats and 1 dog. She would have a zoo if she could afford it! She is a former Science teacher, loves to travel, loves spending time with family and friends, and believes it is important to learn something new every day.

Donna has been an avid reader her entire life. She reads a variety of genres in both fiction and nonfiction. When Donna was younger she wrote short stories all the time for her own enjoyment. She never had the nerve to try submitting them for publication. Looking back, she is glad she didn't! They aren't as good as she thought they were!

A friend introduced Donna to the online indie book community several years ago. Since then, she has been very active in promoting authors. She currently runs Wise Owls PR where she offers proofreading/editing, makes promotional images, and hosts Facebook Events and Giveaways. She does beta reading and ARC reviews for several authors.

Donna is thrilled to be a published author. She has dreamed of becoming an author most of her life but never thought it would actually happen.

www.ingramcontent.com/pod-product-compliance
Lightning Source LLC
Chambersburg PA
CBHW050048230526
45470CB00004B/1443